Introduction

Getting Out Of Your Own Way

W hy do 97% of writers never finish writing their book?

With all the free writing resources available, including online courses, books, podcasts, and blogs, why are so many people not able to finish, let alone start their book?

Does the following sound familiar?

You wake up early in the morning, ready and excited to begin writing. You tell yourself, "Today I will start writing my book. I'm going to be so productive!" Yet, hours later, you find yourself sitting at your desk staring at a blank screen, with no idea where to begin. You have no inspiring ideas coming to you.

Next thing you know, you're googling anything and everything about your topic, which can lead to getting stuck in never-ending research. The days turn into weeks, and then months. Meanwhile, you haven't made any progress on your writing.

You feel lost, helpless, and frustrated. Your morale and motivation hit an all-time low.

Fear and doubt start to creep in. You begin to tell yourself, "This is a stupid idea anyway. No one will want to read my book."

And so you put your ideas on an imaginary shelf to collect dust.

The biggest mistake that all new writers make is waiting for inspiration to come to them, when in fact, they need to chase inspiration.

In this book I uncover the one motivator that all successful authors have in common. It's the one thing that has helped millions of writers start and finish writing their books. It's what has helped me and the eighteen other authors I've interviewed for this book to reach the finish line with our books.

What holds you back?

You may have been writing for months and months but have been making little to no progress. I went through this for years. This cycle of excitement and then getting stuck always left me in doubt. As a result, I began to ask myself,

"Am I 'good enough' to write a book?"

"Who am I to write a book anyway?"

"What if nobody likes what I have to say?"

"What are my family and friends going to think?"

THE WRITERS JOURNEY

How To Get Out Of Your Own Way When
WRITING YOUR FIRST BOOK

PETROS ESHETU

Printed in the United States of America

First Edition, 2021

ISBN 978-0-9985548-3-9 (Kindle)

ISBN 978-0-9985548-1-5 (Paperback)

This publication is designed to provide accurate and authoritative information with regard to the subject matter covered. It is sold with the understanding that the publisher is not engaged in rendering legal, accounting or other professional advice. If legal advice or other expert assistance is required, the services of a competent professional should be sought. Petros Eshetu individually or corporately does not accept any responsibility for any liabilities that result from the actions of any parties.

Inspired Mind Publishing

Table of Contents

"Somebody has already written about my topic. Do I have anything worthwhile to add to it?"

Maybe you have a deep fear of what your family and friends are going to think about your writing. Will you be judged by them? Or perhaps there's a fear of being judged by your peers in your industry.

These doubts and fears can hold you back from sharing your message and making an impact in the world.

What will you get from this book?

After reading this book, you will feel inspired and motivated to write your book. Despite the challenges, setbacks, and failures you may experience, you can persevere and succeed in sharing your story.

When writing their first book, everyone has fears and doubts. It's about moving forward *despite* those fears.

That's why I interviewed eighteen authors and asked them what inspired them to write their first book.

Many of the authors you'll meet are transformational leaders, coaches, and entrepreneurs that have unique messages and perspectives on how they overcame their fears and challenges in writing their books.

You'll also learn

- Your sense of purpose can be the biggest driver in finishing your book.

- How writing is not just about you but about the people you want to serve.

- The importance of having courage to share your unique story with the world.

- How your book's success will be measured by its impact — not how many dollars it makes.

And so much more.

Why did I write this book?

Books have always been my biggest source of inspiration. I love learning and reading the stories of others who have struggled with the same problems I struggle with. Just knowing that someone else has gone on a similar journey helps me feel connected and know that I'm not alone.

Books have completely transformed my life, and I'm always grateful and thankful for the authors that had the courage to share their stories. If it wasn't for their inspiration, I wouldn't be as successful as I am in my life.

That sentiment is what inspired me to write my first book back in 2016. I felt it was my turn to give back to the world that had given me so much. It was not easy, and I faced many roadblocks getting started, but I finally finished it. After that, I went on to write a second book, which became an Amazon Bestseller!

Now that I am a book writing coach, I see those same fears and doubts in the eyes of my clients who share their dream to write a book. They all have mental blocks holding them back from writing. That's why I created this book: for you to have several mentors in the palm of your hand. Whenever you feel discouraged or unmotivated to write, you can turn to the story of the author's struggles and their triumph over them, and find inspiration to stay the course. Writing may be a solo project, but it doesn't have to be a lonely project.

"The journey of a thousand miles begins with a single step."

— Lao Tzu

Chapter 1

Monica Rubombora

Getting Lost In The Details

The first interview I'd like to share was with Monica Rubombora, an experienced managing director in the Management Consulting Industry.

Despite having a plethora of writing resources at her fingertips, she was stuck for many months, making little progress on writing her book.

Something was holding her back. What was it?

Was it that she didn't have enough time to write, or wasn't a good writer?

No, it was something even deeper. It was a negative belief that was no longer serving her and kept Monica from taking the necessary action to make progress on her book.

Are You Making These Writing Mistakes?

What was the biggest challenge you faced writing your book?

I was actually stuck for longer than two months. I reached out to ask for help as I had really been on this writing journey for about a year. I realized that I spent most of that time working on my book title, which is not the right way to go about it. I was stuck on that title idea for months.

When I look at the final title now, it's totally different from what I thought. Also, there were all these doubts when seeing other people's writing and admiring their books.

I was also stuck in doing research for a long time that delayed my writing.

Focusing on the wrong tasks is a common challenge new authors face on their book writing journey. Rather than focusing on the writing, you may work on your book title or book cover instead. Big mistake!

That's not to say that the title and book cover are not important, they are. But they are not important at the beginning of your book writing journey.

Also, many new writers get stuck in a never-ending loop of researching their topics. It's as if you feel like you must do more and more research so you have everything covered and no one can question your credibility.

Monica, who has over twenty years' experience in her industry as a managing director for large multinational technology company, has more than enough credibility.

Having said that, you may have people still asking questions like

- What research have you done?

- What statistical studies did you use?

- Have you included any case studies?

I want you to know that none of that matters.

Unless you are writing an academic or historical book, you need not include all those statistics. It's helpful but not necessary.

All you need is a story that connects you to your audience. *That* is your credibility marker.

Data doesn't move people, stories do!

Accountability Is Essential for Your Success

I asked Monica what she thought was driving her fears and doubts in not making progress with her book.

I didn't feel I was good enough. I didn't feel that I had adequate material for people to see, especially coming from a big consulting organization. I found that I was more concerned about them (former colleagues) reading my work. They're very intelligent people, and I worried about them seeing my work and then judging me for not being good enough or writing well.

Being judged by others is a common fear, especially if it's amongst your peers within your field or industry.

Other fears that can hold you back are

"I'm not good enough."

"What if I fail?"

"What if it doesn't work out?"

Without realizing it, Monica was unconsciously self-sabotaging her efforts to get started. It was when she noticed she wasn't seeing results that she realized she needed help.

I thought I could do this on my own. I had all the materials where I can write a book outline and, you know, it's straightforward stuff, so I would do it on my own. I even got a friend to help me out and hold me accountable, but after about a week or two he lost interest.

I finally reached a point where I needed someone to put a firecracker under my seat so I could be solely accountable. Thankfully, you responded. I felt that I could not let you down. I could not let myself down. It was just that commitment point.

After that, it's like the floodgate opened and ideas were just flowing. It was an immediate mindset change. I started writing. I went back, put the book title aside and started with the outline.

Then I found myself writing, writing, writing, but in between I was getting stuck doing some research. It's at that point at which I met with you for help.

No successful person has done anything all on their own. Everyone needs a helping hand.

"If you want to go fast, go alone. If you want to go far, go together."

— African Proverb

It's All About Making an Impact

I asked, "So what is the goal for your book? What were you hoping to achieve when you launched it?"

I had multiple reasons for launching this book. One reason was to provide a kind of system or process for small business entrepreneurs out there to be successful. Especially if they lack resources or have a small shoestring budget to operate on.

Also, to help them play in this space of business development and writing proper proposals that can help them win business government contracts.

But it's gone further than that now. People tell me much of my information is also relevant for non-governmental organizations because we have a lot of them here (in South Africa) who want to solicit funding from the government for charity type of work. So, this goes broader than just a small business book.

I want to progress from the book and do some online training courses that I would like to develop. This can still assist the same community (small businesses) on improving their own efficiencies.

So those, for me, were the key reasons for the book. It also helps my brand, too, and you won't believe how popular I've become once I announced my book launch to family, friends, and colleagues.

Monica brought up an excellent point.

If you look at her reasons for writing a book, it wasn't because she wants to become an author or establish her credibility or gain a huge following. I mean, yes, that's part of it, but her primary driver was to share her message to a community of entrepreneurs.

I went further, asking Monica why it was so important to help that specific community that she's targeting.

I want to make an impact and contribute. To leave something behind because so much of what I know is from other people. I've gotten here because of others. Everything that I know is because I've walked through it all. I've had opportunities that other people don't have.

So, for me, leaving something long-lasting, like publishing a book on a platform like Amazon, will be there forever. In fact, I've had some people reaching out to me and saying,

"How do you write a book?" and "Is it possible to write a book?"

I say, "yes, it is." It's not as scary as it looks. I love that people are getting inspiration from my path. Also, it's not just about writing books, but it's about goal setting, having discipline and commitment every day to pursue your goal.

I love Monica's response. Sharing knowledge. Making an impact. Leaving a legacy. Giving back and serving others. She's now inspiring others around her to go for their dreams.

Key Takeaways

- Focus on the important priorities for your writing (which is writing!).

- Be aware of self-sabotaging thoughts that may be holding you back from writing.

- Write a book to make an impact and leave a legacy.

To learn more about Monica's book, you can visit Amazon:
Government Tenders (Don't) Suck!: Cut Through the Noise and Win Big Contracts for Your Small Business

Chapter 2

<u>Kathleen Quinton</u>

Is Writing a Solo Project or a Team Project?

T he short answer is both. Kathleen Quinton began her writing journey without help and reached a milestone of 10,000 words. But after that point, she struggled to stay motivated in her writing.

She hadn't shared with others that she was writing a book and was pursuing this goal.

That was until she realized she couldn't do it all on her own. She needed an experienced team to help her cross the finish line with her book.

Are You a Closet Writer?

I asked Kathleen what her biggest challenge was in writing her first book and why she wrote that specific book.

That's a great question. I think my biggest challenge was believing that I could write and publish a book. My "why" for writing the book was that I had something that I really wanted to say. I had been on a journey of self-empowerment for myself for many years. I wanted to help others and share what I had learned along the way. I wanted to share proven strategies and processes that I've seen empower others.

My purpose is to help uplift people. Help people realize that they're worthy and undoubtedly good enough to accomplish their goals. Indeed, to write a book if they want to. Because if I can do it, then anyone can.

The clients I coach are traditionally proactive. They are curious. Learning and growing are non-negotiable for them. A lot of them are leaders. Many are entrepreneurs. I learn a lot as I coach them, and I also realize that many of us have a lot in common.

We don't always know that we're good enough.

We don't know that we're the real deal and capable of accomplishing great things.

An instrumental part of my work as a coach is to help my clients find clarity and self-worth. They can then take steps to move forward and accomplish their goals.

Before we worked together, Petros, I had already written 10,000 words, but I was like a closet writer. Meaning, when I was writing, I kept it to myself and didn't tell anyone for months that I was writing a book.

One of the most significant steps for me was to share with others that I was writing a book. I knew that if I put it out to the universe, I wouldn't be able to take it back. That started to give me the accountability that I needed.

When you get to the point where you're ready, it's beneficial if you can be a part of a like-minded and experienced team.

You may want to work with a coach, find a mentor, or even join a writing mastermind group. I did all of that! As a coach, I believe in the power of setting intentions and taking action on them. There are many nuances to writing a book, and it's great to have an experienced support team that can help guide your steps and save you from having to reinvent the wheel for yourself.

I'd advise those that want to write a book to just start writing. Don't worry about mistakes, typos, your grammar; just get your thoughts out on paper because there are proofreaders, editors, and beta readers that will help you.

This is a great quote that rings true. "You can always edit a bad page. You can't edit a blank page." — Jodi Picoult.

Kathleen shared a lot of great insights.

Many people feel like they have to have perfect grammar and know everything about verbs, nouns, adjectives and all of the writing rules before writing a book. The truth is all you need is your story. Then let the editors do the rest.

Even famous authors like J.K. Rowling or Stephen King don't just write a book and put it out there. They work with editors and proofreaders to produce a book with minimal errors.

We need a team to help us on our book journey. No person has been successful all by themselves. Everyone needs a helping hand.

Need Inspiration? Start with Your Environment.

I asked Kathy what ways or strategies she used to stay motivated in her writing.

I believe in creating an environment for success. I bought myself a coffee mug when I started my writing journey. It has "Begin Anywhere" written on it. It became my go-to coffee mug each morning when I sat down to write. It reminds me of a saying that has always inspired me — that a journey of a thousand miles begins with one step. My goal was to publish a book, and there were many times that goal felt insurmountable. Having a comfortable designated writing area is essential for me. I may light a candle or play soft music. I wanted to do the little things that could help me to stay motivated. A cup of coffee always brings me pleasure, so the mug was a natural fit for my writing environment. The "Begin Anywhere" message helped encourage me. It reminded me each day that no matter what I want to accomplish, I just need to take that first step.

However, the first book can be the most challenging. At the same time, it really is a remarkable journey. It's exciting. It's empowering. But some of the steps can also be tricky, and none of us are perfect. We just have to do it.

Another thing I did for inspiration has to do with the folders on my desktop for my book files. I initially used a working title for my book because I didn't know what my title would be. And then, next to the file on my desktop, I wrote "Bestseller."

It makes me smile to see it. I want to create great books that inspire others. So, every time I see that folder, I do get inspired.

I love how Kathy uses the coffee mug for inspiration. Having inspiration in your environment is a significant way to remind you of your dream goal.

Some ideas I've used for inspiration include

- Writing my goals on sticky notes and placing them around the room.

- Creating a vision board.

- Using inspiring passwords (e.g., IAMABESTSELLER or IAMANAUTHOR).

Also, always surround yourself with people that are pursuing the same goals as you so you can help, support, and inspire each other.

Remember, writing can sometimes be a solo project, but it does not have to be a lonely project.

Who Else Wants to Be Successful Writing in Two Worlds?

Kathleen has written a few books in the vastly different genres of self-help and children's books. I was curious if she was leaning into one genre over the other as she continues her writing career.

'I've been asked that question twice recently. I had an interview about a month ago, and the interviewer said, "So you are a life coach, and now you're writing children's books?" He wanted to know how the two connect.

Well, I am indeed a life coach, and I want to help empower people. I also love children. I have three grown children. I also have six grandchildren whom I adore. There is a great big world out there. Adults want to feel empowered just as much as children can benefit from being empowered. My work is all about emotions, believing in oneself, building resilience, and taking action.

My first children's book is called The Adventures of Quint the Bookmobile: The Big Move to Roneyville. *So there's this very new/young bookmobile that has to move away from all he's*

12

ever known. He has to find the courage within himself to fulfill his purpose.

I believe that we all have a mission and purpose in life.

Quint's purpose is to deliver the keys of knowledge (books) to the people of Roneyville. This takes him out of his comfort zone. He's doing something extraordinary to serve his community. The second children's book has a theme of friendship and sharing.

That's very much what I work with in my coaching world.

Basically, Kathleen wants to write books that help people develop qualities that focus on believing in oneself and serving a purpose for adults as well as a younger audience.

Another significant point Kathleen brought up was the importance of having a reason, or "why," for your book that's bigger than you. There's no way you will finish your book if the focus is just on yourself. You have to look beyond yourself.

Kathleen said she was writing her children's books to share mindfulness themes for all children while also keeping her grandchildren in mind. That's what gives her fulfillment in writing her books.

Absolutely. That's how I tie it all in. So, I haven't left my personal development role at all. I am a life coach, and I love that. That's a passion for me, and so is writing children's books. I believe all writers are strategic. We want to impart a message. We want to contribute and make a difference. Whether I am writing for an adult or a child, I hope for a positive outcome for my reader. If we can help children to believe in themselves at a younger age, I think they will discover their purpose earlier in life. I am tying it together that way. It makes me happy. I feel both genres align with my mission. I feel like both are a perfect fit for me.

Key Takeaways

- Surround yourself with a team of supporters in your writing journey (don't be a closet writer).

- Set up your environment for success.

- Don't be afraid to share your message within different book genres.

To learn more about Kathy, visit
https://www.quintessential-coaching.com/

Chapter 3

Kevin Desrosiers

A Book Is About Serving and Not Just Making Money

I n this next interview, you will learn how Kevin Desrosiers, a retired electrical engineer, had procrastinated on writing his book for many years until he finally ran out of reasons and excuses.

It's About Overcoming Adversity in Your Life

I began by asking Kevin how he got into writing in the first place.

I retired a little over a year ago, but I'm not your typical writer. I was an electrical engineer by degree, and engineers aren't known for their writing ability. About fifteen years ago, I came up with the idea for a book. It's based on my family's story and my first father-in-law's story.

My dad grew up in Rhode Island, but his parents emigrated from Canada from around Montreal. He served in the Air Force. That's where he met my mom. My mom had my sister and me, but without a high school degree or college degree, my father found it hard to get great jobs. Our family did okay, but we were poor by most standards. My dad said, "Enough of this, I've got to do something about it." He earned his GED, then he used a GI bill to get an electrical engineering degree in college.

For the better part of about three years, my sister and I barely saw him because he was working during the day to support the family and going to evening classes to get his degree. By the time he got home from class, my sister and I were in bed.

Both my parents sacrificed to make sure my sister and I had everything we needed. He broke the chain of poverty in our family because his family grew up poor.

Also, with my first father-in-law, the only reason he was born in the United States is because his mom was in Arizona picking crops. He got citizenship that way. When he got married and started having children, he made sure that all nine of his children spoke English and valued education. They were really poor, so they had the children working as early as possible. All the money went into the family, and their big treat on Friday night was to go to the store to buy a gallon of ice cream and some root beer to make root beer floats. Every one of his children turned out to be successful in life.

I saw that as an inspiration for me as I got to know my father and my father-in-law. That's what inspired me to write a book about people that have overcome adversity in their lives. That's what my book is about. I have interviewed twelve people who have faced extreme adversity in their lives. Each chapter is about somebody that has faced adversity and overcome it.

Adversity is something that we all face and can relate to. It comes in all shapes and sizes, which is why I love that

Kevin's book includes people from all walks of life sharing their stories.

We all are going through the same storm, but not all of us are in the same boat. It's insightful to hear different perspectives.

Overcoming Challenges that Hold You Back

I asked Kevin what writing challenges he faced while writing his book.

I basically had three challenges, and I think I've overcome them all. One challenge was procrastination. I had the idea for this book fifteen years ago.

I always had excuses as to why I couldn't do it. I was still working a full-time job (fifty to sixty hours a week). I had things to do and "this and that" in my life. I always found a reason not to start the book. Even though I told some friends I was doing it, every time they asked me [how is it going?], I would shut up. I got tired of hearing that.

After I retired a year ago, I was going to a Christmas party at a friend's house. He's one that asked about my book every time he saw me. In December, right before his party, I got together with a couple of other people and started working on my book with them. So, when he looked at me when I walked in the door, I said, "I know what you're going to ask. Guess what I just started?"

It was just uncomfortable with people asking me, "How's it coming? How's it coming?" I put it out there. I think that it's good to put it out there. But what it really got me was, after I retired, I ran out of excuses. Now, when my friends asked me, I couldn't say,

"Well, I'm working fifty to sixty hours a week," or "I have other obligations."

So that was my first challenge. That was just getting over the hump.

The second challenge was fear.

I had never written a book before, and I was afraid of what the editors might say or what people would think about what I wrote. When I finally got off the dime and wrote the first chapter, I sent it to my editor. That was hard because I was still coming up with excuses.

I couldn't write at home because there were too many things going on at home. Every time I sat in the house, I knew this repair had to be done, or the doorbell rang, and so on. I had to overcome those things. Those weren't really obstacles. They were just fears in my mind. When I finally got that chapter to my editor, he had a lot of edits. But overall, he told me to "just keep writing the way you're writing because you write well."

I had a fear about my writing, but now that I've received that feedback from my editor, I feel good! I know I'm not perfect, and he gave me a list of things I need to work on. But at least now I've gotten over that hump, and I know I can do it. That was huge for me being able to do that.

The last thing that really has been a problem for me is environment. I talked about writing at home. My kids are moved out, so one of the bedrooms is converted to my office. I don't write in there now because, for some reason, no matter how hard I try, when I sit there and try to work on my book, I just can't do it.

So, I've done two things. One, I found a place that makes me forget everything else in my life. I went to the local library where *they have what they call study rooms. I go there and use an individual study room.*

The thing that really got me over the hump on my first chapter, and this might be expensive for most people, is I booked the hotel about 90 miles from my home. It was a suite-type hotel that had a kitchenette in it, so I brought my food. I brought my pots and pans even though they had theirs already. I just hunkered down inside that hotel room. I stayed there for two full days and just wrote. I told the front desk I didn't want a maid service. I didn't want any interruptions. That was just really a big jump start for me. That got me going and got the ball rolling.

For me, just getting in an environment that is different from my everyday environment was crucial, and now I've just got to be consistent. Going off to a hotel or a cabin or whatever can get expensive. I'm hoping the library works better. But if that's what it takes, I want this book bad enough. I'm going to do it.

Then, COVID hit and the library and hotels were no longer an option. I found an online writing group, Shut Up and Write, and tried a session with them. Basically, you meet via Zoom, say what you are working on that session, then everyone shuts off their sound and writes for an hour or two. At the end, everyone reports on what they accomplished. And guess what? It allowed me to overcome my phobia of writing in my office at home! I started attending several of these every week, and now my book is in the final editing stages.

Kevin was determined to overcome his big challenges including procrastination, fear, and environment. Sometimes we have to think outside of the box to accomplish this, but it can be done.

Kevin brought up an important motivator for some authors, which is telling others about his plans to write a book. I think that's key because it gives you some accountability. Even though it took Kevin a long time to take action, it was that accountability that reminded him and pushed him to start his book.

> "Accountability is the glue that ties commitments to result."
>
> **— Bob Proctor**

Serve Others with Your Book

I asked Kevin what he hopes to achieve from this book.

Well, I just hope that anyone that reads it gets some inspiration. If they're battling with some sort of issue in their lives, they can tell themselves, "You know what? I can do it," because this is about everyday people.

The people I interviewed for my book aren't celebrities. These are people that my friends have introduced me to. People with different types of stories. I have somebody that overdosed on drugs, somebody that was trafficked, somebody that has PTSD, and even some that were homeless. I'm covering as many different types of struggles as I can for people, so that anybody can read a chapter on what they want. I'm hoping somebody reads the book and says, "You know, my situation is bad, but I can do it because this person in this book did it. I'm just like them."

That's what I'm hoping.

Kevin is not writing just to be an author or for status; he is doing it to inspire others and to showcase the stories of people from all walks of life and how they've been able to overcome their struggles. He wants to help you change your perspective of your problems and to help you know that you're not alone and that others have walked in your footsteps and have succeeded. There is a light at the end of the tunnel.

Kevin shared one last thought.

I have a lot of experience speaking through Toastmasters, now I can contact several organizations that help people with struggles, those that help the homeless, people with drug issues or alcohol issues or people that have had different adversities in their lives. I'm volunteering to speak at these locations. Hopefully, I'll sell the books in the back of the room, but if it's a poor organization, I'll give some of the books away. The main thing is to help people. I understand as an author, very few people are going to get rich off of books, but for me, it's going to be a fulfilling thing where I help somebody else. If I break even, I'll be ecstatic, and if I don't, then it's not the end of the world. I'm doing this because it's something I really want to do and to honor my parents for their sacrifices in life.

Key Takeaways

- We all have unique backgrounds and stories that can inspire others.

- You need to tackle your writing struggles head on and overcome each obstacle.

- Writing a book is about serving others and not just making money.

***

To learn more about Kevin's book, visit
https://www.bridgeoveradversity.com/

Chapter 4

Sanae Floyd

What If My Book Is Rubbish?

The next author I interviewed was Sanae Floyd. She is a business breakthrough coach who helps entrepreneurs and business owners identify and connect with their ideal audiences.

Writing a book was a recent project for Sanae, and she had so many doubts throughout her writing journey:

Is it good enough?

What if no one reads it?

Will I look stupid in front of people?

All those doubts went away when she received a piece of advice that forever changed the way she saw her writing. Writing was no longer a "should" but a "must."

Why Everyone Must Know About Book Structure

I asked Sanae to tell me about her biggest struggle with writing her first book.

I think structuring and organizing my ideas was the biggest hurdle, and just the whole planning process.

I had the backbones (commitment) because I wanted to publish the journal of my own journey.

But the first stepping-stone was, when I consulted with you and you advised me to look at having three major themes that form the beginning, the middle, and the end. That structure was helpful.

Lacking structure was the biggest thing. I really struggled with thinking how is it all going to fit together.

Sanae was fortunate that she loved to write and that she always made the time for it through journaling. She had the habit of journaling her experiences with her challenges.

Sanae had already written her material, so all she was needing was structure and putting it together in a way that made sense. This is a common problem for new authors.

Where do I start? When do I end?

This is why having an outline for your book before you begin to write is crucial.

An enormous advantage of journaling is that it captures your story in a raw format. In other words, you share your feelings about your experience in the moment. It is fresh on your mind.

You can see this in the famous book *The Diary of a Young Girl,* in which a 15-year-old Jewish girl, Anne Frank, hid with her family for two years from the Nazis that occupied the Netherlands.

Anne Frank journaled her feelings and experience, and you can see and feel her fears as if you were right there with her back in the 1940s.

One Piece of Advice that Changed Everything

I asked Sanae if she had any writing challenges or negative beliefs that were holding her back when thinking about writing her first book. She answered:

I remember talking to a lady who had published a book probably about a year before me.

I said to her, "How do you know if [your book] is any good? And how did you know that people would like it?" I asked that a few times because I kept thinking, "Well, how do I know if people like my book?". It might be rubbish.

It was something that she said to me that I will not forget:

"You've got to think of your book as a manual. You've got to see it as a personal development book."

She continued, "Write it as if you're writing it for yourself. You are just putting it out there. It's your process. It's very personal. If others like it, great! Just trust that it's good enough."

That was helpful to hear. To have that kind of set mindset. To know writing this book was my process and my own journey.

As a result, I just told myself "I'm just going to trust that I'm proud of this piece of work, and hopefully other people will like it too.

I love that answer from Sanae.

See your book as a manual, as if you are writing it for yourself. Know (and trust) that if you like it, then others will too. This is a great mindset to have.

Whenever I coach a new author to write a book, the first thing we work on is developing an author mindset, and by that, I mean developing the right goals, rituals and habits to help them in their writing. So when, not if, doubts and fears pop up, they have tools to handle it.

You don't wait to be an author to have an author mindset; you need to have an author mindset to be an author.

Why You Need Purpose for Your Book

Sanae wrote a book about debt. I was curious why she decided to write on that topic and not something else.

After all, she has a successful coaching business, so why wouldn't she write something related to that business? For example, a book related sales, marketing, how to run a business, etc.?

Well, it's quite a personal journey. The book is about overcoming the emotional burden of debt, which has been a challenge I've lived with for a long time.

I lived with the emotional burden of debt for 23 years.

Before I conceived the book, I had made a decision that I needed to break this pattern that was holding me very small. I was suffering in silence, and there was a lot of shame around it.

I decided that enough was enough. I was going to break this pattern of debt, and that I would get myself out of debt.

I was working with a mindset coach at the time, and we talked about really needing a bigger purpose (for getting out of debt).

The thing that came to mind was, "If I do this, if I can break this pattern of debt that I've lived with for a lifetime, then this stuff needs to be shared.". As a result, the purpose became a real driver.

There were moments where I just wanted to give up ... sometimes I felt like living with debt was easier than working through a plan.

In those moments, knowing that if I actually paid my debt, then I could share my journey helping others overcome debt. That was such a compelling reason to keep going.

Sanae had the purpose and mission to share her experience with those who are struggling with debt.

Writing the book was no longer just about but about being an example to other people that needed to hear and be inspired by her story to overcome their own debt

For most readers, just knowing that someone else has gone through the same burdens is in and of itself reassuring because it helps them know they are not alone in the struggle.

People are not looking for anecdotes or solutions as much as they are seeking connection.

Having debt is a sensitive subject as there is a lot of shame and guilt that comes with it. Most people avoid the money topic and sweep it under the rug.

It's just one of those subjects that is so sensitive. I was talking about this recently with some friends, about how you can be in a

dinner party and talk about how they met their husband or wife and really hear intimate details about the family.

However, you try asking about how much money they owe or how much debt they have, and you will never get invited back to that party again. Debt is just one of those unspoken/taboo topics. So, it felt like a very important topic to write about. That's why this had to be my first book.

Key Takeaways

- Have a structure for your book before you write.

- See your book as a manual for your life that others can use.

- Have a purpose for your book beyond yourself.

✱✱✱

To learn more about Sanae's book, you can visit Amazon: Paid in Full: Free Yourself from the Burden of Debt and Live Your Best Life N

Chapter 5

Lorraine H. Tong

Don't Know Where to Begin?

Many people don't know that in 1939 before WWII began, a 24-year-old American journalist by the name of Alan Cranston had recently returned to New York City from Europe and shockingly discovered that Adolf Hitler's book *Mein Kampf*—as published in the United States—was heavily sanitized and did not reflect Hitler's true intentions for global expansion.

Using Hitler's own words from the original Nazi manifesto, Cranston translated and wrote an annotated, condensed edition to expose the full measure of Hitler's evil ideology, chilling anti-Semitism, and plans for world domination.

This was all detailed in a short historical non-fiction book written by Lorraine Tong. I was fortunate enough to interview Lorraine to discuss not only her book but the whole process of capturing this significant piece of history.

Researching a Book is an Adventure

I asked her to share the biggest challenge she faced in writing this book.

The main challenge was finding the time to write because I have family and a full-time job. I wrote at night and on weekends, and a few times I actually fell asleep on my laptop.

Because it's a historical book about a real person in history, it was imperative to be factual and true to Alan Cranston's memory. The core of Hitler on Trial: Alan Cranston, Mein Kampf, and the Court of World Opinion *is about facts and the whole truth.*

Alan Cranston is very well known in California and represented the state for 24 years in the U.S. Senate. He was a Senate leader and candidate for President in 1984. His life's mission was to stop the nuclear arms race. I was his foreign policy legislative aide and advisor for eight years.

To write this book required that I conduct extensive research to give context about Alan's unique role in exposing Hitler during his rise to power.

To make Alan real to readers, I included some of his childhood stories, talked to his family, and delved into his extensive collection of papers in Berkeley, California. In those files, I discovered the young Alan Cranston and what shaped him into the young journalist he was, his travels in Europe, and what inspired him to expose Hitler.

His son Kim and daughter-in-law Colette were very generous with their time and supportive of my project. I was honored to be invited to their home where Alan lived the last years of his life. I was given a chance to examine Alan's library, which had remained almost untouched since he died in 2000. They showed me Alan's original copy of his annotated, condensed version that he wrote. That was an absolutely thrilling moment. After my book was published, I was stunned to find a copy for purchase on eBay. If you read about the court ruling chapter in my book, you'll understand my amazement over this discovery after 80 years.

Research is an adventure. Tracking down the court records that shed light on the lawsuit that Hitler's American publisher brought against Cranston's publisher/partner for copyright infringement was a worthwhile pursuit and provided credibility. My book reintroduces Alan Cranston to not just one generation but probably two generations.

It is said that it takes a village to raise a child. It took a team of historians, authors, and friends to provide me with valuable feedback to birth my book. I am grateful to them for their expertise, insight, and generous time.

What an experience to research someone's life and the impact their work had in the world. I love that Lorraine shares an important part of history that the world might have not known, especially our generation.

Sharing someone else's story can be just as important as sharing your own. Lorraine raised a good point: when capturing historical events, you must do extensive research in order to be factual. Thankfully, she saw this research process as an adventure in discovering the truth.

Want to Write a Book? It Starts with Commitment.

I asked Lorraine how long she had been wanting to write a book and why she felt this should be her first book.

My love of books led to a love of writing. It was a natural progression. I wrote a historical romance novel when I was fourteen, which will never ever see the light of day!

When I came to America, I was six years old and was the only person of Asian heritage in the whole school in Palo Alto, California, and I couldn't speak English. As a result, there was a lot of pressure to learn quickly. So every day after school, I'd watch "Rawhide," and on Saturday mornings, I watched the old classic Tarzan movies. I am grateful to Clint Eastwood and Johnny Weissmuller for helping me learn English. I rejected the stereotype of the Asian student who excelled at math. I concentrated on learning and improving my English, but I kept up my Chinese because I was always proud of my heritage.

The book I really wanted to write for decades was about my grandfather, who was secretary to Dr. Sun Yat-sen (who led the 1911 revolution that changed China from dynastic rule to a republic, and became its first President). My grandfather helped him draft the "Three Principles of the People" (nationalism, democracy, and livelihood of the people) and raised money for the revolution in America. This is my current project.

However, Alan Cranston's story became the priority because I could still interview his family and others who knew him. I had thought about writing this book for over fifteen years. I had asked a good friend, who also worked for him, to co-author the book, but she was unable to collaborate due to family obligations. The necessary intensive research began only a year before I began to draft the book. I thought about the way I wanted to structure the book and the highlights long before I actually began writing."

Lorraine waited a long time to write Alan Cranston's story. The challenges she faced in the research were finding people or family members who could speak about the past event(s) or the person (or both) as well as finding books or documentation that captured the historical events.

The author is now using her research experience and writing a book on her grandfather's legacy that extends all the way back to China's 1911 revolution.

Lorraine's journey is a reminder that a book is not something that you just dabble with or take a half-way approach. If you decide to write a book, you need to be fully committed. It will take an enormous amount of time, so make sure the time is well spent.

I've learned the hardest part about being an author is not physically writing your book but rather making the decision to write it. Once decided, you just need to get out of your own way and things will start in motion.

Self-Publishing: Do You Really Need It? This Will Help You Decide!

Why did you go the self-publishing route instead of using a traditional publisher?

I could have taken the traditional route, but a publisher would want me to promote the book and travel on book tours. I cannot do that because of my full-time job and family responsibilities.

But the main reason for self-publishing is because I had a very clear vision of what I wanted my book to be — the focus, content, structure, etc. There is more control in self-publishing. I believe more people want to read shorter books, and my intent was not to write about Alan's entire life.

The truth is, it's actually harder to write something short rather than the luxury of writing a longer one. [I think] it was Mark Twain or Hemingway who said, "If I had had more time, I would have written you a shorter letter."

Also, I had another challenge (just to add a level of complexity), which was to provide the context of history for the audience. After all, life was so different in the 1930s compared to today. How far did I need to explain the world as it was at that time? Because once you go in one direction, a traditional publisher or editor might want me to expand this or that part or cut and remove other parts. Then the length of the book could become too long and unmanageable. It would have been more difficult to keep the integrity of the story and set boundaries and the limits to the scope.

Looking back, I underestimated not only how difficult it was to write a book but also to complete it. Along the way, I realized that I also must learn how to promote my book. Marketing is a whole different skill. I learned to write and direct a book trailer to keep me laser focused to finish the book. The trailer gave me momentum.

Lorraine brought up a good point on how self-publishing her book was the best route for her because, unlike when using a traditional publisher, she can control how her work is presented.

She controls her creativity in terms of its focus, how to organize it, when to launch it, how long it will be, etc. Traditional publishers have more say in your book's content and how it should look, which may or may not align with your vision.

Also, many new writers underestimate the amount of work it takes to finish a book or reach a goal. You will encounter obstacles along the way that you may not anticipate. Embrace them!

Key Takeaways

- When writing a historical book, view the research process as an adventure.

- If you decide to write a book, make sure to fully commit to it.

- Find out if self-publishing or traditional publishing is best suited for you.

To learn more about Lorraine's book, visit
Hitler on Trial: Alan Cranston, Mein Kampf, and The Court of World Opinion
and book trailer:
https://www.youtube.com/watch?v=-5jY0H-Uajc

Chapter 6

Gabriela Casineanu

How to Turn Inspiration into Success

Imagine that you get so burned out from work that you can't talk anymore... your voice disappears!

What do you do?

This is exactly what happened to our next author, Gabriela Casineanu. A few years ago, she was going through a very busy time hosting daily workshops and dealing with many clients. Overworked, spending too much energy and not enough time to recharge (for an introvert like her), she got to a point where she lost her voice for a few months.

How scary is that!

Some people would have crumbled in the face of such a challenge, but she took it as an opportunity for growth. As a matter of fact, not being able to talk inspired her to write her first book... and the writing process triggered her recovery from the burnout.

Opportunity or Challenge? They are the Same!

I asked Gabriela to tell me about her biggest challenge writing her first book, in terms of what myths or beliefs she had that may have stopped her from writing.

That's a very interesting question. I did a presentation to fifty people who were interested in writing books, and one asked the same question. For me, it was a bit different from what you're probably expecting.

I went through a burnout in 2016. I couldn't talk for four months, and many other health issues showed up (lack of focus, barely walking, anxiety and panic attacks, always tired...). Alarmed by not getting my voice back within two weeks (as normally happens), I got worried and asked myself one day: What will I do with the rest of my life if I can't talk anymore?

Unexpectedly, the next thought hit me: "Write a job search guide for introverts!" I never thought about writing this book before. Where did it come from?

By that time, I had a decade of experience in applying coaching to employment counseling, and I had helped thousands of people. But I never thought to write a book about this topic.

When that idea came to my mind, it made sense. I have the experience and a lot of stories of introverts successfully applying the strategies I've developed. Coming from a coaching viewpoint, I bring a fresh perspective that usually is not captured in employment counseling books.

What was even more interesting was the energy that accompanied that thought.

I experienced that energy before, several years prior to the burnout. I dislocated my knee during a ski trip. While going through the recovery process, the same type of energy accompanied the thought that came right after a dream: to emigrate to Canada. Trusting the energy would bring something good, I sent my application and came to Canada — even though my knee was not fully recovered (I was still not walking normally). I love how my life has unfolded since, so it was an excellent decision.

I recognized the same energy with the thought of writing the book. I was like: It worked that time (to come to Canada), so let's see what capturing my knowledge and expertise in a book will bring.

Anyway, since the burnout had such a toll on my health, sitting and writing on my laptop was something I could do, at least in small quantities at the beginning. Since even focusing on something was a challenge at that time, I started with ten to fifteen minutes. I wrote a few sentences, stopped. Wrote again, stopped. Immersing myself in this process also helped regain my ability to focus. I gradually increased my writing time and ending up writing seven to eight hours a day by the time I finished the book nine months later. And the next month, my self-published book became a bestseller in seven countries.

It's inspiring to hear how Gabriela was going through a rough period in her life with a burnout but took that as an opportunity to pursue an idea.

Rather than seeing the situation as negative (and feeling down), she turned it into a positive. In life, sometimes you have to jump into a new project even if you feel you're not ready and you don't know how it'll turn out.

How to Turn Your Challenges Into a Super (Writing) Power

I asked Gabriela what other writing challenges she faced in writing her book and how she overcame them.

Three more challenges:

I'm a Romanian-Canadian, not a native English speaker. But since my idea came to me in English, I decided to write the book directly in English. Sometimes I had to double check if the meaning was what I meant to say. Other times, it was quite funny. I was surprised by how easily the words were flowing from mind to "paper," even words I never used before (although I knew their meaning). I discovered that writing is a creative process, despite the genre we choose

Since I had no experience writing a book, I had to rely on what I've accumulated along the years: skills and experience in engineering, IT, quality assurance, program design and coordination, business, and coaching.

So I problem solved my writing by creating an outline for the book. I started by writing a book proposal and creating mind maps to help me structure the ideas I wanted to capture in this book. Then I grouped the ideas in chapters and ordered them in a way that takes the readers through a transformative journey (instead of just dumping information into their mind). My business experience came in handy, as I treated this book as a product. I didn't have to just design (write) the product, but also create and build momentum before launching it, then promote it during and after launch to reach more people.

Since my workshops were very interactive and experiential – and I wanted to offer the readers a similar experience through this book — when I started writing I wondered how I can do this in a written format. By the time I got to those chapters, I came to trust the creative process; putting my worries aside made "space" for the idea (of how to create a similar experience) to present itself.

Talking about creativity, the book turned out quite different from what I envisioned at the beginning. Although I already had most of my content, the writing process helped me to present the ideas in a better way. Two new chapters (new content) crystallized while going through this process that made the book even better.

Gabriela shared a lot of wonderful things here, like the fact that she used her background and in engineering as part of her creative process.

She solved her writing challenges the same way she solved problems in her engineering job. She organized and outlined her book to provide structure so it's easy to follow and read.

What skills or talents do you already have that you can apply to your creative writing process?

- How do you get organized? What type of brainstorming do you do?

- How do you keep yourself accountable?

- What projects, either at work or hobbies, have you completed from start to finish? What can you learn about yourself from those projects, and how can you transfer those skills to your book project?

Reflect on these questions.

Following up, I asked Gabriela if she used other techniques in her creative process.

I think life prepared me to write that book. If I look back, it's like life gave me the right experiences to learn what I needed to write and get this book into the hands of those who might benefit from it. That built my trust that I could handle writing this book.

Using music helped me get in the creative flow every time I sat down to write. As someone usually very active, I couldn't just stay at home. I tried different places to see what worked best for me and discovered that Starbucks is my best "writing office." I went there to write almost every day. Sometimes, at Starbucks, people are talking around you. To stay focused on writing, I put my earbuds on and listened (on repeat) to one of my daughter's neoclassical compositions for piano (Candlelight Memories). It's relaxing and worked like a charm, creating a space between the outside and my inner world, which facilitated my creative process.

Writing long hours brought pain to my eyes, and it became difficult to continue typing. The soreness went away when, as advised by another author, I started to use the EyeCare Chrome browser extension. It signaled me to take a break; when prompted, I stopped to do some eyes exercises, stretch and even dance a bit. Why not have fun?

Don't Just Sit There, Follow Your Gut

I asked a last question: Why did she feel that writing a career book for introverts was important over any other book?

I didn't even question the idea because I didn't start by wanting to write a book and then looking for a topic. When the thought came to me to write a guide for job searching for Introverts, I said, Okay, let's write it. It was also intriguing, since I was already interested in helping introverts more but never thought to do it through a book.

I have worked with a lot of introverts, and I know they need a different approach for job search than extroverts, which is not usually found in job search books. It totally made sense to use the energy of that thought and get the book out. The bonus – getting my health back by the time I published that book – proved that the burnout was a blessing in disguise. When I was writing, I really felt that the book was pushing me to get it out into the world as soon as possible (without knowing why).

The best part? Writing that book made me fall in love with this creative process and started my writing career (sixteen books so far, and counting). I had no idea that I would start writing before that thought. So for me, that book was just a starting point to a new enjoyable path.

I love the fact that the book just came out of Gabriela. She knew many introverts needed to hear her message. There are lots of books but very few that cater to introverts on this topic. Being an introvert herself, it made perfect sense for her to target that audience.

- How about you? What topic would you like to write about?

- Is there something about that topic that no one else (or only a few) has written on?

- Can you offer a unique perspective?

Key Takeaways

- Face every challenge in your life as an opportunity to grow.

- Look at your current skills, talents, and knowledge to see how you can apply them to your writing.

- Listen to your gut when deciding what your first book should be about. Or, like Gabriela, ask yourself the question and stay open to receiving the answer!

To learn more about Gabriela's book , visit Amazon

Introverts: Leverage Your Strengths for an Effective Job Search

Chapter 7

Elsa Mendoza

Cast Away the Doubts

H ow do you handle all the doubts and fears that pop up on your writing journey? Because it's not a matter of "if" but "when."

The next author, Elsa Mendoza, tells us the different ways she handles doubts and fears. It doesn't matter whether you're writing your first book or third, there will always be those fears and doubts that linger in the back of your head.

Elsa also shares the importance of having a reader's mindset as you write your book and the importance of setting an intention before you start any kind of writing.

Why You Are Your Best Cheerleader

I asked Elsa, "What challenge or belief did you have about writing that held you back from finishing your book? And how did you overcome it?"

Dealing with imposter syndrome, including all the doubts and negative thoughts in my mind. I've experienced it especially with my first book as well as in my second and third books.

Thoughts like:

"Who are you to write?"

"You're not famous [enough] to write."

"Who's going to read your book?"

"English is not your first language. It's only your second language."

Still, you have to believe in yourself. All these thoughts you hear, they are not true.

So if thoughts are telling you, "Hey, you can't write that," or whatever it is, just ignore it. Believe in yourself. Have confidence. Just keep writing.

You are your own encourager, and you are your own empowerer.

It's your responsibility to believe in yourself, to take care of yourself, to love yourself, and to appreciate yourself.

When you're writing, is someone prompting you? No. Nobody's prompting you, it's just you. You and your heart and your new manuscript. So just believe in yourself. Continue writing. Ignore the negative thoughts. I've experienced all of that from the first book up to the third, but I just kept writing.

Elsa raised a good point regarding imposter syndrome, or the fear of not being good enough to do what you are doing (or want to do).

I can relate. I didn't think I had what it took to write my first book. I never thought it was even possible to write and publish your own book. Thankfully, I had a book coach who believed in me, and so I used her belief in me to get started. Slowly, I built the confidence to believe in myself.

You cannot remove thoughts. These are just thoughts that you can let slip by, but they are also energy. So, once you are consumed with a particular thought, a negative thought, for example, and you add more stories, later on, what will happen is it will affect your emotions, so you'll feel bad. Then, when you feel bad, it will start to affect your behavior and your attitude, your work, and the people you meet. And so, instead of having a good time, you're having a bad time.

It's all because of that single thought that you have entertained in your mind. So you have to be careful, especially in writing.

I still feel like a newbie writer every time I write a manuscript. I still go through that imposter syndrome.

But just ignore [those doubts and fears], keep writing whatever it is, and believe in yourself.

Write as a Reader (Not Just as a Writer)

"How did you know what book to write first?"

I didn't know what to write. It was actually my husband who told me, "Duh, Elsa, your quotes," because I've been writing quotes here and there. To self-publish is just one of those things on my bucket list, and it sat there for quite some time.

So, I decided to start with the quotes (book), but how was I going to write that? I didn't want just quotes but a bit more. There should be a story how this quote came about, right? That's the reason I included the short narratives for each quote because I wanted the readers to concentrate on the quotes, and then let them reflect and interpret them. Every reader has his own interpretation.

So in the short narrative, I included my story, how it came about, my insight, observation, and experience.

But what about the reader? How are they going to interpret the quotes? Are they going to get the same interpretation?

When I write, I'd like people to reflect and look within themselves because I'd like them to realize the power within them. I'd like them to know that we are people of power, peace, and joy.

When I write my books, I position myself as a writer but also a reader.

I agree with her. I also position myself as a reader and as a writer.

When I write, I think of someone that I'm close to and pretend that I'm writing an email to them. This allows me to be my authentic self in my writing and have a casual, conversational approach.

It's true. Like I said, I position myself as a writer and a reader. As a writer, I'd like to write something that will be so inspirational that this person will really improve her or his life. I'd like to help a person realize their power.

As a reader, I'd like to see a book that's not preachy and imposing. I'd like to read a book full of encouragement, where I'll really be moved.

That's what's happening when I'm writing. That's the journey that I'm on: a writer and a reader. These are the self-talks.

People don't always want more information or strategies but rather are seeking connection. If you can't write or understand what your reader is going through, then how will you begin to make a positive impact in their lives? People want to be understood. You do that by meeting people where they are in life and guiding and inspiring them in a new direction.

Are You Intentional with Your Writing?

I asked Elsa to share the one piece of writing advice that she can give to somebody who's just starting out and might not know where to begin and is feeling overwhelmed.

Number one, it's okay not to know first. No one is in a hurry, so just relax. It will come to you. I didn't know what to write first. My husband saw me in deep thought for a few days asking, "What am I going to write?"

It's okay if you don't know, it will come to you. Ask the Universe – the Universe or God, whatever you want to call it. It will be shown to you; it will be given to you. Plus, I think it's a lot better if you find your intention first. Know your intention, your purpose, and then from there, you will have the idea of what to write.

I love the idea of setting an intention before you write. To know that it's okay if you don't have all the answers. The ideas will come when they need to.

You could also ask or brainstorm ideas with people around you. What's important is to have an intention or goal for your writing before you begin.

I think everything boils down to intention. It guides you, positions you to where you want to be and where you want to go. There's a lot of clarity when there's intention. Not only in writing, but I guess it applies in all that we do and say. To know, ask yourself, "Why am I writing this?" You have to know your "why." You have to know your purpose.

It all boils down to intention.

If I post something on my social media accounts, I always go to my innermost, to the core, to my awareness to ask myself:

"What is my intention?

"Why am I going to post this?"

On my Instagram account, where I always write poetry quotes, I ask myself first,

"So what's the intention behind this?"

"What am I sending here?"

"What kind of message?"

"Will this benefit humanity?"

I'm really careful about that.

There is already a lot of pain and suffering in this world, so you don't want to add more pain. You just want to be an encouragement to all; you just want to be an inspiration to all; you just want to be an enlightenment to all. Bring some light, bring some encouragement, bring something for people to be excited about their lives.

That's what I do. That's the intention of my book.

Key Takeaways

- You are your own best encourager.

- Always consider the reader's perspective.

- Be intentional with any kind of writing you do.

To learn more about Elsa's book, visit Amazon
You Can Quote Me On This: Words to Empower You and Awaken Your Consciousness

Chapter 8

Tony K. Ansah

Healing through Writing

The next author I want to introduce to you is a poet, a social entrepreneur, and a blogger. His name is Tony Ansah. He shares his experience in discovering the self-publishing world that gave him an opportunity to share his poetry and other writings from the last decade. Self-publishing fulfilled his dream of one day becoming an author as well as leaving a lasting legacy for his kids and the younger generation.

A New Way to Publish a Book

I asked Tony to first tell us about the biggest challenge he faced when writing his first book, and if there were any limiting beliefs or myths that he had about writing.

I would say as far as myth is concerned, there's only a traditional route you can take for your book. You give it to the major publications to see if they'll be interested in publishing your work. However, I went the unconventional route. Once I came across [self-publishing], I did some research and homework to see the overall process. After taking some notes, I then explored doing it myself.

I learned as I went along. Fortunately, I had a lot of content to pull from since I've been writing poetry for a long time. I would say probably for at least fifteen years or so. I had a full catalogue of material to pull from.

I selected the most relevant content I could pull (the ones that stood out). I put together a compilation of my poetry, which I then divided into a five-part series.

There is a common belief that the only way that one can publish a book is through a traditional publisher.

However, as Tony mentioned, there is another option to publish a book that is becoming increasingly popular: self-publishing.

In terms of self-publishing a book, an author writes a book and completes or directs the entire publishing process — drafting, editing, designing, and formatting the book — without the aid of a traditional publishing company.

You will oversee the entire book writing process from start to finish, at your own expense, and with full ownership of your book rights and full control over the end product.

Tony already had content to use from the years he had been writing, which gave him a bit of a time advantage, but don't be discouraged if you have written nothing in the past. Most new authors have to start from scratch, including myself.

Writing Is Therapeutic

I asked Tony to share how he determined the main theme for his book.

Most of my content comes from my personal experience, my upbringing, and how I was raised. I'm an American immigrant; my parents are from Ghana. I was exposed to their (Ghanaian) culture and that tradition, so that was my reference point, and a lot of my poetry is related to that. It is very therapeutic for me, as I feel like I'm in a peaceful place when I write.

I also write about positive aspects of my life. It's really about inspiring others. It's about motivating others to be the best version of themselves. I touch on how you can achieve your dreams and goals to be successful in life. I come from a very positive place with positive thoughts and energy. That's kind of the perspective I bring and what inspires me to write.

When writing, you want to bring your unique perspective to your work. When you have a message that only certain people will connect with, you find your tribe, your group, your people that connect with your message more quickly than trying to adjust your message so it appeals to everyone.

I love how Tony mentioned that writing is therapeutic (that's so true) because it's not like you sit down and put pen to paper with no emotions involved. It may appear that way, but there are a lot of feelings and emotions that bubble up when reflecting on the past. Sometimes when you write something down, you have the opportunity to acknowledge the past and what you went through.

Acknowledging the emotion attached to a painful event is the first step to healing.

That's how I approach it. Regardless of whatever I'm writing about, it's a form of therapy. That's the process I bring, as far as my thoughts, my views and how I analyze the world.

Leaving a Legacy

When writing a first (or second, or third . . .) book, you have a goal in mind. I asked Tony what his goals were and what he hoped to achieve with publishing his first book.

I wanted to test myself to see if I would be able to self-publish it and go through the process from beginning to end. I always had an interest when it came to books, even during my high school years. I always was interested in having my own bookstore, for example.

I looked forward to the day where I could actually have my own book, with my name as the author. So when this opportunity came along to self-publish, my main goal was to just put together this book and share my thoughts.

I wanted to share my perspective with the world, to have something that I could pass on to the next generation — whether it be my children, the youth, or whomever. So even if I'm not here, this is still a book that showcases or highlights who I was when I was here. That's how I see it. Just an opportunity for me to be able to share who I am and my experiences [in a way] that will be able to stand the test of time, whether I'm here or not."

Tony could not have said it more beautifully. We all have a book within us. A couple of years ago, I wanted to write a book but thought it was impossible to get started. The thought of pursuing a book deal through a traditional publisher was daunting. Then, I met my writing mentor who introduced me to self-publishing.

I, too, knew that this was an opportunity that I had to take. I also wanted to leave a legacy for my future kids, grandkids, or the next generation, even though I haven't met any of them yet. I wanted to ensure I could share my life lessons and values, so they would know who I was and what I stood for.

Essentially, you're writing a book for yourself. Lessons that you wished you knew in the past. Stories of overcoming any of life's challenges you faced.

If you have a life event or something significant that takes place and you're able to document it, whether it's on the spot or as soon as possible, follow through on that. While it's still fresh in your mind is the perfect time for you to put it on paper and release it. Once you go through that process, revisit it. See if there are other thoughts that come to mind that you would like to add.

For me, I let it sit and marinate for a bit and then revisit it at least three or four times before I can settle and accept it for what it's worth and then move on to something else. But sometimes, you let the spirit move you, you write down what comes to your mind, and then you let it simmer a bit. It's almost like you're cooking something, and you add the necessary ingredients and flavors to season it so it will reach a point where it's ready to be shared. That's how I see it.

Key Takeaways

- Self-publishing is a great option for publishing your book versus going the traditional route.

- Writing can be therapeutic and a form of self-healing.

- Leaving a legacy of your work for the next generation is the best gift you can give.

To learn more about Tony's book, visit Amazon
Diary of a Ghanaian Diaspora Entrepreneur

Chapter 9

Otakara Klettke

Your Key to Success: Consistency

T he next author is Otakara Klettke. Her first book became an International Bestseller, and she sold 10,000 copies in the first year.

Despite her huge success, you may not know that she had a lot of doubts and fears writing her first book, especially since English isn't her first language. She had many difficulties on her writing journey, but it was when she reached a milestone in her life that she started and finally finished her first book.

Writing Is Like a Muscle that You Need to Exercise Every Day

I asked her what the biggest struggle was when writing her first book (or any of her books).

The first book you write will be the biggest struggle because you're stepping outside of your comfort zone. You have no idea what you're doing.

It's like you keep walking forward in the darkness and the ground lights up as you step down. But when you walk this path again (in other words, write another book), it's already lit up.

There are still the same struggles, the up and downs, no matter whether it's a first, second, third, fourth, or even my fifth book that I'm working on. There are moments where I think the book is awesome and you celebrate,

"Woohoo! It's so cool. I love it. This is going to be the best book."

Then two days later, you crash. "Oh, nobody's going to read it. Who's going to believe me? Nobody would ever want to read what I wrote."

You go through this roller coaster of emotions.

However, once the roller coaster of emotions happens on your third book, you're like, "Okay, cool. This is my downside. I feel bad. I will feel better again about it later on."

So you know that these waves will come and go. Now, I know when I don't feel super good about some part of my book, all I have to do is move forward, even if I have to struggle through it.

I love Otakara's approach to writing.

As a writer, you will go through ups and downs (as with anything in life). You are not always going to feel like writing every single day.

Some days your motivation will disappear, and you really have to push through.

There will be times where you question yourself.

"Is anybody going to read this?"

"Who wants to even listen to me?"

Those thoughts are going to happen on and off, and it's just about moving forward, weathering the storm, and letting it pass.

It's like when you go exercise: you go to the gym and when you're exercising, you're going towards the end of your last sets of reps. You're tired, but if you've exercised before, you know that even though you're tired, you're going to feel better afterwards. If you keep doing it (the exercise) more often, then it becomes easier. However, if you want to challenge yourself, you will always challenge yourself to where you're exhausted.

But with books, sometimes it's hard because you're in that process for months. You're not in that process for a day or two; it's something that is taking a much longer time. But once you go through it and work on another book, it will get easier. And if your book is unsuccessful, then so what? You have a chance to write another one. But it's important to just do it.

Having the Courage to Share Your Story

I went on to ask Otakara what beliefs or myths she had about writing before writing her first book?

I think the biggest one was that I would have to have great English to write a book. I had lived in the United States for fourteen years by the time I published my first book. I'd learned English way before at school and had traveled the world already.

I always wanted to write a book as I always was good at writing. I felt like a writer at heart. I always loved books.

I don't speak my own language, which is Czech, good enough anymore because I don't use it enough where I could write a book in it. I felt like my English wasn't substantial enough to write a book in English, until I was told, "You'll get an editor."

Then, my first book was my own birthday present for my fortieth birthday. I wanted to turn the decade with something meaningful, something that I would do.

I truly wrote a book for myself. The book is meant for people, but the reason, the core "why," was just for me. It was my own present to myself. I gave myself permission to suck. I was done being a perfectionist. I decided to write a book, and I would expect nothing out of it. I wasn't putting any stipulation on a book.

I was just thinking, "If I get this published, I'll be happy."

Well, not only did Otakara get the book published, but she also became an international bestseller.

I asked how that felt.

It just floored me. I was really successful with my first book becoming an international bestseller. I didn't even know any marketing, and it sold 10,000 copies in less than nine months. I was not even advertising the book. It just went out, and people were talking about it, and people were contacting me about the book.

The book really resonated with people. It was a great thing because that helped me to want to stay in the book industry.

It helped and encouraged me to go on with other books. However, it also made me afraid to write a book in the same genre, because I thought if I want to write anything else, I'm going to disappoint someone because the bar suddenly existed so high.

I published three other books, now I'm working on a fifth book that is going back to the same genre of my first book. It took me publishing three other books to gain enough courage to face my defense of that first book and continue to write on that same subject. So the doubts are there.

Right before you publish your first book, you're terrified. I don't think there is a more terrifying feeling like you're at the edge somewhere looking down and you've got to jump. You're just going to be exposed. You're going to be out there.

The feeling of actually publishing, it's worth the entire journey of getting there to launch it and bring it to the people because the book all of a sudden gains its own life. You're bringing some magical force into the world.

I can relate with Otakara as I also had a fear of exposing myself to the world. I was a typical shy introvert that loved to hide in the background, and now here I was writing a book. Everyone would know what I thought.

Like Otakara, I too came to the U.S. about fourteen years ago, and even though my English was good speaking wise, my writing sucked. Getting the right grammar or punctuation was a challenge.

However, my motivation for finally writing a book was that I wanted to leave a legacy of my work for my family. I realized that if I died, then nobody would remember I existed except my immediate family and friends.

I wanted to leave my work so that even future generations could see it, including my grandkids and great-grandkids. Even if I don't meet them, at least I can share my life lessons with them through a book.

What Everyone Must Know About Feedback

I asked Otakara if she had any other writing advice to share with us.

If I could give any advice about anything to first-time authors, it's just to know that the struggles happen. They're real, and they happen to everyone. They will happen even in the future. But the key point is to move forward.

It doesn't matter if you hate your book or you don't like what you're writing at that moment, just keep moving forward. Because once you keep moving forward, there will be the point later when you will get a chance to fix it. But if you get stuck in that moment, I can promise you will never ever get out of it. That happened to me during editing with my first book. It took me four months to edit my first book. It was brutal because I wasn't used to getting a critique back. I took everything too personally.

When I write now, I give my books to beta readers, which I didn't do with the first book, but I get my book critiqued many times before I even bring it to the editor. Now I'm okay, and I understand I'm exposing myself, but I don't take it personally anymore. I just want them to give me feedback. Getting the feedback for the first time, though, that was the hardest.

This advice reminds me of a great quote I use, "Feedback is the breakfast of champions," by Ken Blanchard.

Getting feedback in any work you do is always hard at the beginning, whether it be in your writing or at an office job.

When you're giving your book to the editor for the first time, it feels like you're giving them your baby. It is a creation that came from you. For somebody to criticize it, even though its constructive criticism, is still hard to take. You have to get past that negative feeling because to become a better writer, you need feedback.

No matter how good you are, there is always room for improvement.

Also, know that feedback doesn't speak about you as a person or about the quality of your book. What's important is sharing your message.

Otakara gave another piece of writing advice.

Another advice I would share is to keep your book on your mind. If you're serious about your book, then you know that you're going to finish your book. That's all you can think about.

When you go to sleep, you think about your book.

When you wake up, you think about your book.

Throughout the day, there is not much time that you think about anything else. You're doing your job, you go to work, you're with your family, you're with your kids . . . but there is still the book. It's somewhere in the back of your mind.

Allow the space for it.

Allow the space to inhabit the part of your heart, inhabit part of your brain, and just inhabit part of you. Allow that book to be there both through the struggles and the good times. So that would be my last piece of advice: Don't forget about your book.

That is a good piece of advice to let your book occupy your mind along with the other things in your life. Let it be part of you. Let it infuse as part of your life, just like adding sugar to your tea and stirring it to the point where you can't tell the difference. That's how your book journey will be. Let it be a part of you that you can't separate from.

Key Takeaways

- Exercise your muscle in writing by working at it every day.

- Have the courage to share your story with the world.

- To become a great writer, you need to be open to feedback.

✳✳✳

To learn more about Otakara's books, visit her Amazon Author Page

Chapter 10

Ariston C.M.

Don't Downplay the Significance of Your Story

O ur next author is Ariston C.M. She's a coach, a speaker, and a business owner. She has a homecare agency that services persons with developmental disabilities. As you can imagine, she has a lot on her plate to juggle, but yet she finds the time to write.

You may be in the same boat as Ariston. Maybe you're running a business or working 9–5 along with taking care of your family. It can be a struggle to carve out time in your day to focus on your writing.

This author shares her lessons on time management along with having the courage to share your story.

You Find (or Make) the Time to Write

I asked Ariston how she finds time to write in her busy day, and if she has a writing schedule that she follows.

I have a schedule, but not really, because I don't like having to set time to do stuff. Every day I have something different that I work on. I'll devote maybe an hour or two to certain projects. I call them my personal projects. Then for my business, I have to work on it daily. I'm about to start another business, so I just kind of go in order of importance.

Of course, the businesses are important because that's what's bringing in the money. However, writing and helping people is my passion.

I have three or four other small projects that I need to work on. So, I don't sleep much. I sleep an average of four to five hours a night. Late at night is when I work on my personal projects.

It's impressive how Ariston is able to accomplish so much in a short time. She makes full use of every waking hour she has. It's easy to make excuses and say that we don't have enough time to write or to work on our dream goals. This author makes the time. Everything she does is intentional. She does not leave it up to chance.

It reminds me of a Jim Rohn quote: "Either you run the day, or the day runs you."

I asked Ariston to elaborate on how she prioritizes her tasks. That's something a lot of new authors have difficulty with.

When I first started writing my book, I would get up a half hour earlier than usual, and that was my writing time. I was able to write my entire book within thirty days. That did not include all the edits and everything else.

When I went to my second book, I worked on it here and there, but I got tired of having those remnants. So for one night, I stayed up all night long. I refused to go to bed until I sent my completed book to my editor, which was about 7:30 a.m. I just take the time and I make it work. It's important, and I know that I have a message that people need to hear, so I'm going to make time for that.

Inspire Others Through Your Story

Ariston wrote *The Courage to Dance Again,* which is based on her story and overcoming the pain she went through that eventually led to finding her purpose.

I asked Ariston why she felt she needed to share that message in her first book.

For me, it was healing. It was me moving on. It was me really addressing and looking at those issues that have shaped my life for so long. I knew that other women could benefit from it. I knew how I felt, and I didn't want any other woman to feel that way.

We're gonna make mistakes. I can't save everybody. Some people who read the book before they even get in those situations I went through can save themselves from a lot of pain and suffering.

I got an email from a girl who said, "I think you just saved my life." That's all she wrote. That's why that book was important. I needed to start with that message. It told people who I was and how I emerged, as well as how I am and who I am now. I felt there was a very important message that needed to be conveyed first."

Instead of being selfish and keeping her story to herself, Ariston wrote her book to serve others. What good is knowledge if it is not shared?

Don't get me wrong, it takes a lot of courage to be vulnerable and open up about your story. However, that is one of the first steps to both self-healing and building connection with your reader.

A repeated theme you will read throughout this book is that you are your own ideal reader. You know the pain, the pleasure, and the struggles that another person may be going through.

You can speak the words that your readers need to hear to heal. It makes the whole book process worth it, even if it's just helping one person. You could save a life.

Don't Hold Back in Sharing Your Message

I wanted to know what Ariston's biggest challenges were in writing her first book.

Was there a belief or myth she had about writing or publishing that held her back? How long had she wanted to write a book? Also, what was the biggest challenge or belief she had that was not true?

I've always wanted to write a book. I keep a prayer journal, and I have an entry dated in 2007 that says, "Lord, helped me write this book from your heart." I kept trying and trying to write the book. My computer crashed, and I got discouraged. So, I left it alone for a number of years.

It was when my business crashed that I was at my lowest place. I had nothing left. What better time to write the book? My biggest challenge was deciding what information to put in the book — there was so much of my life that I had to leave out. I had to really decipher what was important to include and what was not.

I was excited and I've always written great work (it was natural). A lot of people think it's too hard and they can't write. But, once you set your mind to it, the words just flow.

I appreciate Ariston being vulnerable, sharing her struggles and how she had been wanting to write her book for years. Sometimes it takes reaching a low point in your life to realize the opportunities that you have around you.

When you have nothing to lose and are at rock bottom, the only other direction you can go is up.

Finally, I asked her to share a writing tip especially for someone who doesn't feel anyone will listen to their story.

Know that you have a voice. Everybody has a story, and you don't know who needs to hear yours. You can't downplay the significance of the things that you went through, or the ideas that you have, because somebody somewhere needs to hear that — no matter how insignificant you think it is.

Your book is not going to be for everybody, but it will be for someone, so don't allow that to discourage you. You have to step up to move forward and grow. If a person were to follow through with writing a book, that would have a big influence in their life and in the lives of others. It will give them that confidence that feeds into their significance that can push them to go bigger and do better things.

Key Takeaways

- Be intentional with your day and setup your writing time.

- Share your message because you never know whose life you might impact.

- Have the courage to pursue your dreams.

To learn more about Ariston's book, visit Amazon
The Courage to Dance Again: Finding Purpose in Your Pain

Chapter 11

Paul Lowe

The Power of Owning Your Story

Paul Lowe is our next author. He has made a remarkable transformation from living many years in dark, desperate despair to living a healthy, happy, and fulfilling life now. In this interview, Paul opened up about his past and how he overcame his challenges. He also shares one of the big reasons why people don't want to write a book.

Your Past Is Not a Reflection of Your Future

I asked Paul to share why he wrote his book.

We've all got a story. I'll tell you my story now. It's a true story. It's captured in one of my books, Emerging from the Forest. *But I think it's important before I unfold that story to really reinforce that it's just a story. It doesn't define who I am, what I am, or what I've done in the past, or what I'm likely to do here and now, or in the future. It's a story.*

That's very important because I think as people we get bogged down on this whole identity of who we think we are and not who we actually are. Who am I? That simple question has kept me inspired and intrigued for most of my life, and I've got the answer now.

Going back to my childhood when I was a young guy, six or seven years of age, I lived with my grandmother and my mother. We led a very simple but poor life, but I was happy because I had two beautiful matriarchs in my life. I also got a beautiful mongrel dog called Rocky, who doubled my world, and I was just blissfully happy.

All that changed when I was eight and my mother remarried. Things changed dramatically. We moved away from the city into the countryside. I hated every second of it. I hated being dragged away from the certainty of all I'd ever known and the love of my grandmother and dog.

In a matter of weeks, it became very apparent that my mother's new husband was not a nice guy. What started off as initially sort of shouting at my mother, shouting at me, nothing was ever good enough, criticizing, and complaining very quickly turned into abuse and then mental cruelty. In no time, it went into physical beatings for both of us. This has all happened within twelve months.

I went from this kind of blissful existence to this horrific nightmare. That prevailed on and off for four or five years.

I found some solace in something called Nottingham Forest Football Club. I thought that one day I would play for that football club as a professional player. What I didn't realize at the time is what I call the power of beliefs: to have that belief, to have that focus, to have that direction gave me a real sense of purpose. Despite the fact that everything around me was falling apart, I had something in my sights that gave me a reason to keep going. I believed in that football club so much that they were my everything. If they won, I was absolutely elated. If they lost, I was beyond despair. They controlled my life, and I didn't even realize this. Every second of every day, I was dedicated to that one thing.

Eventually, I detached myself from the belief that they were my world because I think it's extremely dangerous when you look externally for something to control your life. That control comes from within. But it took me decades to learn that lesson.

Paul's story about the challenges he faced at a young age and the drastic changes he had to adopt is so inspiring. All of us have a story to share. It's difficult to be vulnerable and share your past and what you went through, being afraid of what people might think or of being judged. That's why I love what Paul said at the beginning, that it's only a story and it doesn't define who you are.

Let Life Happen Through You, Not to You

Paul shared the difficulties he had writing his book. I was curious if reflecting on his hurtful past slowed his writing progress.

Is what it is. I've got no emotion attached to it because it's the past. I take the learning from it and move on. It doesn't make me happy. It doesn't make me sad. I think there's great learning in that.

Thank you for asking that question because I think there's a massive life lesson in the answer. That is, all events in life are neutral. The only power they have is what we choose to give them. Now, obviously, as a child, I didn't have the intellectual capacity, experience, or knowledge that I've got now.

It's like when we eat or drink, we take the goodness out of that consumption, and we pass the rest as waste. It's the same for life; when something happens, let it happen through us, not to us because if it happens to us, we'll keep it there and become spiritually and emotionally constipated, and then we will die. That's what happens. Take the goodness out of the experience, which is called learning, and pass the rest off as waste.

One of my mentors said to imagine a life where the TV screen is you as the higher self. Characters will come on screen. They will come and they will go. Some characters in the drama will be happy and some will be sad. These things come and go, like the seasons come and go. But the one thing that remains constant is you. You are the thing that's never changing, not being influenced by these characters. The character that I was as a child is no longer the character that I am today. In a moment, time will be no longer. The wind is passing through all the time.

It's about having that awareness to observe these human beings living in this moment doing what we're doing on this screen.

In a moment, that will be gone. But the screen will still be there.

I love that analogy of how we are a screen with different characters. Characters will change but you the screen will always remain the same. We're always redefining ourselves. Who I am now is different than who I was a year ago or even a few months ago. Also, I loved how Paul frames all events that happen in life as neutral, and that it is how we interpret those events that can lead us to suffer.

By the time Paul wrote his book, he already had the breakthrough, acceptance, and awareness of his past, and understood that his past and his story don't define him.

Therefore, he is no longer attached to the negative feelings of those past experiences.

I think a lot of people struggle or feel ashamed of sharing their story. The feelings are too strong when they think back on the past. What's ironic is that the very thing that you don't want to put in the book is usually the very thing that you need to add in order for you to heal: to face any shame, fear, guilt, anger, and disappointments, and to let it all stay where it belongs, in the past. Again, you can decide at the end if you publish it or not.

Living with Purpose

How can someone bypass the fear of sharing their story?

Very good question and I have a simple answer. There is a quote by Tony Robbins, "Your past does not define your future," which is a very general kind of response. But when I look back and make sense of the whole journey, my life's purpose, I've done some deep dives on a lot of stuff over my journey. But to keep it really simple, it's wrapped up in purpose. What is our purpose? To understand why we are here? "Who am I?" To understand that and accept it? As individuals or as human beings, we make mistakes, things happen to us. But again, let them happen through you, not to you. That's the difference.

We're here to serve, all of us. We have to pay rent for being on this planet. Part of our rent is not paid in dollars or sterling or euros. It's paid by the contributions we make. There are no free rides in life. Some people would wrap this up as karma. Just be careful of what energy you put out there.

The fact is, things might have happened in your past, like murder, rape, violence, or whatever. If it's been part of your journey, embrace it. Be grateful for it. Because you take that learning out, and that has helped to shape you for the beautiful soul that you are. If there are a lot of lessons from the experience, that's great. You can become a massive teacher for people that may be going through the same thing because you've got the credibility of knowing what you're talking about and inspiring others accordingly.

New writers starting out sometimes get stuck on the edge and don't want to share their full story. They think maybe no one's going to listen to them or their family and friends are going to judge them. Remember, your story is part of you, and the past does not define your future.

Key Takeaways

- Own your story because no one else will.

- Let life happen through you and not to you. Detach from your past.

- Your story is what gives you credibility, no one can take your story from you.

✳✳✳

To learn more about Paul's book, visit Amazon
Emerging From The Forest: From Pain to Purpose (Mastering the Game of Life)

Chapter 12

Ling Agaran

Stay Focused on Your Dream

Our next author, Ling Agaran, had always dreamed of being a makeup artist. For the last ten years, she has spent her weekends grinding to get her makeup business off the ground while also working her 9–5 job.

Despite all the challenges she faced in her life, she remained persistent towards her dream and never lost focus. Now, she is a successful international makeup artist, and she decided to give back by sharing her story through a book with the hope of inspiring others to dream big and to never give up.

Inspire Others with Your Story

I began by asking Ling to share what inspired her to write her first book.

Well, I came from the Philippines and moved to Canada when I was twelve years old.

I'm the only artist in my family. They don't really understand the mentality of an artist. So when I went into this field, I was ashamed because I felt like I had to be either a doctor, a lawyer, or an engineer to be successful in the eyes of society.

Society tells us to be successful in those professions, but I went into the makeup artistry because that is my genius zone. I help people feel good about themselves. It's not being vain. It's more than skin deep. It's expressing your individuality as a person. I knew that at a young age, and makeup became my passion.

The whole limiting belief with makeup artists is the struggle to keep bringing clients in consistently, because no one's going to come in to get their makeup done every single day. It's not like a haircut, either.

Therefore, we have to find a 9–5 job or a second job to make ends meet, and our makeup artistry becomes a side hustle. Makeup artists stay there for a really long time and don't know what else they're supposed to be doing. When you focus on a 9–5 job, you tend to move away from your passion because you're not putting the energy or focus into it anymore. I've never lost it throughout the years.

I've been a makeup artist for over ten years. I had a 9–5 job working in the medical field. That was my weekday job, but I would come alive on the weekend when I worked on my passion.

So the struggle for me was the fear that if I left my job and started doing makeup, I didn't think I could make it in the world.

Now Ling works on her business full time and is an international makeup artist who works with clients from all over the world.

Often when we look at success stories, they seem to have happened overnight. On the contrary, most successful people have been putting in the work for years before the result of that hard work is visible to everyone else.

Many times, you need to get a 9–5 job to pay the bills while you work on making your dream business become a reality. I love that Ling wrote a book to help inspire others who are still struggling in their journey. To give back. To let other makeup artists know that with persistence, determination, and focus, they can have their dream business too.

What's the Worst that Can Happen?

I asked her what beliefs or fears she had about writing when she first began.

It's that fear that comes and haunts me all the time when I start a new journey. I actually secretly started writing this book because I'm such a private person. It's really hard to put yourself out there. We're in a digital world where you're not only reaching people in your community but also globally. So when I started writing a book, it's like "I'm really going to put my story out there?"

Know that, when you put yourself out there, you need to be prepared for backlash or haters of people. You're not going to please everyone. I needed to look at all the fears that I had.

I would start to ask the question, "So what if no one likes what I have to say?" Then I would answer myself. "Well, if no one would like it, then it's normal and it's natural. Because I can't please everyone. So, what is the worst that could happen?"

I kept saying that until I came up to the worst thing that could happen. And really, in the big scheme of things, there isn't anything worse that could happen. That's how I kicked my fear.

When I wrote this book, I wrote three chapters on fear. I was going through a lot of personal struggle at that time already, but as I went back to read those chapters, I was so proud of it. I felt like I was reading someone else's journey. I felt like as I was reading it, I could relate.

This author brings up a good point on fears that can pop up such as "What will people think of my writing?" It takes a lot of courage to be vulnerable to share your story.

Ling used a powerful exercise to get rid of her fear. What if the worst-case scenario happens and people don't like your work? What will happen?

Your story is yours to own. What people think of it is none of your business. Your job is to simply put your message out there in the world.

It's unrealistic to think your story will resonate with everyone, but those people who your story resonates with will be your biggest fans.

Don't Tie Your Value or Self-worth to the Outcome of Your Book

Next, I asked Ling what she hoped to get out of her book and what her goal was.

I honestly wasn't thinking of what I wanted to get out of the book. Even now, I'm actually not hoping for anything. Again, this is not about me. I took myself out of it a long time ago.

Isn't it self-centered to think "What if no one likes me? What if people don't like what I have to say? It's all me, me, me?" But it's not about me. It's about the people I want to serve. When you come to a realization you should put other people first, it becomes about them.

I wrote this book for makeup artists. I wrote this book for anyone out there who's struggling to start their business or is having all this doubt. In life, we can take on someone else's limiting belief and make it our own. I want to put a message out there that others' limiting beliefs do not have to be yours.

It's so true that we unknowingly pick up limiting beliefs from other people.

"You can't do that."

"You can't go for your dream."

"You can't make money from your passion."

Hearing that from someone you trust can have disastrous effects on your progress. It can hold you back from your dreams for weeks, months, or even years.

Another important point Ling mentioned is to have an intention for your book that focuses on others and not yourself. The goal for her book was just to put it out there. She then detached her value from the outcome because she has no control over what others think of it. The people that find value in it will read it and those that do not won't.

Key Takeaways

- Inspire others with your story.

- What is the worst-case scenario for writing your book? Question it.

- Don't tie your value to the outcome for your book.

To learn more about Ling's book, visit Amazon
Little Miss Slay: How One Makeup Artist Made Her
Dreams a Reality

Chapter 13

Tiffany Areco

Don't Let Age Hold You Back From The Author Within You

Next I would like to introduce you to Tiffany Areco, a Bolivian writer, who discovered her love for writing in her teens. She enjoyed reading and writing stories, and she even joined a few writing competitions. Despite not winning any writing contests, she ended up getting help self-publishing her own book at a young age. Now as an adult, she shares the lessons she's learned along the years and the importance of sharing your story.

Writing Has No Age Limit

Because she published at a relatively young age, I was curious to know how Tiffany got into writing.

Well, the first book I ever wrote, was when I was eighteen years old, but it got published when I was twenty-four. When I was young, I knew I was going to be a writer. I used to read a lot, and

I wanted to share and create the amazing worlds that I had in my mind.

But the chance for publishing a book came a long time ago. It came after I wrote a book for a contest in my country (Bolivia), but I didn't win. I said, "Okay, why not try again?" I tried two or three times with different books, and I still didn't win anything.

I ended up going to self-publishing and crowdfunding. There were people that liked my book and helped me publish it. I have it now on Kindle, and I'm very proud of that. Then I stopped (writing) because I didn't want to share any other fantasies. Instead, I wanted to be able to help people because that's what I want to do now. I know that's my true calling. So, I'm preparing myself to have more knowledge and things to share.

It's impressive to see how this author wrote a book when she was eighteen years old, and self-publishing a few years later is icing on the cake. I would not have known at that age where to even get started with publishing.

Now Tiffany wants to know that she is touching people's lives. When you write a book and someone buys it, you don't necessarily know if the book was impactful in their lives. But when you're going out there and you're serving others and meeting them face to face, it gives you instant fulfillment in the work you do.

Right. For example, the book that I wrote [and published] is a children's book. It is about the life of someone that found a box. I wanted to share part of my story of what I've been doing. I want to help women think outside the box and know that they can do other things and they don't have to put limits on themselves. Because whatever you want to do, you can do it. That's why I stopped writing and decided I want to share a message. It's vital to let yourself free to be what you want. You can let yourself create these places and situations that you want. I'm trying to give this idea that, as you can create fantasy worlds, you can also create an idea or an ideal world for yourself.

Writing Is a Marathon (Not a Sprint)

I asked Tiffany to share the biggest challenge or belief she had about writing.

Something that I am still working on, even this moment, is that when I was younger, I used to say "I write only when I have inspiration or when great ideas come to my mind."

I believe that I am very blessed because my mother is a teacher, so she always gave me books to read and always told me that I can do anything. That's something that I'm very happy and grateful for. Also, I got to meet this student who was preparing himself to be a writer too. He was studying literature at the university, and I was just finishing high school.

I asked him, "How can you write so many books?" He gave me a book as a gift and in it there was a line that said, "A writer is not someone who writes only by inspiration, but a writer is someone who knows how to write." He told me that you must prepare yourself, train yourself. It's like a muscle.

He would write every day. The first day he would write only one paragraph. Then the next day, two paragraphs, and then the next day, a page. You just keep working on it like that. I found out that when you exercise your brain, and you create this kind of habit, it will be easier for you to put your ideas in writing.

My challenge at first was that I didn't have great ideas, but that wasn't true. I just didn't have all the words or the knowledge to just write them down. If you want to be a writer, you have to sit and write every day. Also, I believe that writers have to read a lot, because that's how you're going to find better expressions and better chances to express an idea like you want to. When I was younger, my vocabulary wasn't the best. I started listening to other people and how they express themselves, so I could see if I would find a better way to share my idea.

Tiffany is right. We all have inspiring and amazing ideas to share that can change the world. This is not the first time I have heard the idea that writing is like a muscle you need to keep working. Learn to just show up and write every day. Even if it's ten to fifteen minutes of writing or writing just one paragraph.

Start where you are. Like a snowball going downhill gets bigger and bigger, the same applies to writing. Every day those paragraphs turn into chapters, and you will have a book done in no time.

The Curse of Knowledge

When asked about the one writing tip that she could share with someone who's telling themselves they aren't good enough or questioning if anyone would listen to them, Tiffany had some great insight.

I believe that when you are trying to share anything, the first thing that you have to focus on is that you have an amazing story to share. I believe that all of us have a unique story.

There's something inside you that needs to be told to the world. You are unique.

We are all relatable. Even if you think "I'm just a housewife taking care of my kids," I believe that you have lived something that could be useful for someone else. So, my only tip is to trust yourself. We have amazing things to share with the rest of the world. Just be yourself.

Also, you want to make sure you write about what you know. I will not write about something if I don't have a close relationship to it. The book I published was a children's book that I wanted to share with one of my family members. I was thinking about her when I wrote it. The other books I wrote were more for a young adult audience, so I imagined all my characters were people in their mid-twenties.

Many people don't believe in themselves. Like Tiffany mentioned, they don't believe they're special because they think, "Oh, I'm just a housewife," or "I just work this 9–5 job." But if you live long enough, you face obstacles, and the fact that you're still here means you have a story to share. This is often called the "curse of knowledge" in which you have learned so much that you paradoxically think you know less than what you actually know. We know more than we are led to believe.

Everybody is unique, even though at times you might not feel it.

You may want to write your book, but you might think nobody's interested in hearing what you have to say. That is not true—you have a purpose for your existence, and an untold story that could have a positive impact on someone's life.

Key Takeaways

- You can start writing at any age.

- Part of being a good writer is just showing up to write. Write at least a line or 2 every day.

- Don't be afraid to share your unique story.

To learn more about Tiffany's book, visit Amazon
La caja de Giacomo

Chapter 14

Christine Fonseca

Learn How this Dynamic Author Writes about Her Passion

T he next author, Christine Fonseca, differs from the other authors I interviewed because not only has she written seventeen books (which is a lot!), but she's done it through traditional publishing as well as self-publishing. Despite her success as an author, what you may not know is that it took her five years to finally write her first book.

"Who Am I to Write A Book?"

Because she has authored so many books, I asked Christine if she had always wanted to be a writer, if that had always been her passion.

Well, the answer is yes and no. When I was a kid, I started writing little tiny stories in kindergarten all the time. I remember this great story about a mythical woman. Her name was Unitess from Atlantis. She came out of the ocean, and her job was to unite the whole planet. I wrote that when I was five. I've always written stories, but somewhere along the line, I decided that wasn't a real job.

I had modeled when I was in high school, so I thought I'd live in New York, maybe I'd pursue that. That was a struggle and was a really hard hustle. I realized that's not what I wanted to do.

In college, I had this vision of sitting in a coffee shop in New York City writing books and fantasized about what it would be like to be an author. I had that always kind of in my head, but I just never really pursued it.

Many years later, my husband and I wound up moving back to California and we were considering having a family. There was an educator crisis in California, a shortage of teachers. My husband went to do his undergraduate with the idea of becoming a teacher, and I switched my career and became a school psychologist.

Years later, our school district asked me to teach some parenting classes. I specialized in gifted children because my own children were gifted. I'm a gifted adult, and my husband was gifted in his own right. I researched it. I specialized in that area and people kept saying, "Wow! Christine, there are no books on what you talked about, you should write a book." I was like, "Yeah, yeah, whatever." But I kept hearing from people, "Hey, there are no books on what you're doing, you should write a book."

This went on for five years.

Finally, in 2008, I was like, "Hey, you know what, I should probably write a book about this stuff." With a lot of encouragement from my family, that summer I said I would write a parenting book about gifted children. The second I said yes to that in my life, imaginary characters took over my brain. That summer, instead of writing that book [about gifted children], I submitted my first novel.

What a story of Christine's life and the journey she took to discovering that she was an author. It's like she knew in the back of her mind that one day she would write a book. You might be in the same space where deep down you want to write a book but you get busy with life and doing other things. Maybe, like Christine, people come to you saying, "You should write a book about this or that. . . ."

I asked Christine what beliefs held her back for so long.

"Who am I to write a book?" That's really what it was. I think my own story of trauma from my childhood — I'm an adult survivor of trauma — I think that all played into it as well as this denial of that artistic part of me, and really understanding that there was no reason to ever deny that arts are an actual job, and artists are really important people on the planet.

I truly believe artists are the observers of the world. It's the artists' job to show up in a society and observe everything, to comment on everything, to shed light on dark spaces and the places people don't want to go, and to share stories about that.

Through the act of stories, either your own or somebody else's, or some fictional characters', you get to see different humans showing the good, the bad, the ugly, and everything in between; to show the universality of what we go through in our shared human experience; and to do that through storytelling.

I believe passionately in the power of stories to heal and to shine light on dark places and the power of the artist to tell the story that people are unwilling to grant otherwise.

91

Don't Hide Your Gift from the World

We touched on this a bit earlier, but I wanted to know what made Christine finally make the decision to write a book.

I think the reason I finally decided I was going to sit down and write a book was because of a need to serve. A calling to serve. I had spent the last five or six years really noticing that there were no resources to speak of for parents of gifted kids and that parenting gifted children was a different experience from parenting children who are typically developing. I felt like there needed to be more resources.

I've always had this gift of being able to read complex subject material and distill it into something completely palatable for anybody, to make it seem almost simplistic and bring it down to its essence. That's always been a skill of mine, so who am I to not use that skill? Who am I to not share that if that's truly a gift? The need to serve outweighed any barrier I had to writing a book.

Also, when the fictional characters showed up and decided they really wanted to tell their story, it was such a compulsion. It was such a high to get into the fictional stories of these characters that I couldn't do anything but write. It really wasn't an option. It's never really been an option.

When something is your passion, it's very difficult to avoid it. It's a part of you that can't be separated or denied. It's what gives you life, happiness, and excitement. That's your zone of creativity. That is your artistry. What it ultimately looks like will be different for everyone.

It's important to discover your gift, so you can serve the world with it. That's what gives you lasting fulfillment, just as Christine is fulfilled by writing books and sharing her artistry through fictional stories.

Commit to Just Show Up and Write Every Day

There is a lot of talk about having a "why," or purpose. Is having a big "why" the primary motivator for writing, and should it be? I asked Christine to share her perspective.

Totally. I have a course called "Soulful Writing" that I do specifically for non-writers, like spiritual entrepreneurs and what not, who want to write a book but don't even know where to start. The first section of that course is all about "Why do you want to write a book?" Don't write a book because somebody told you to write a book. Don't write a book because some guru out there said to do it. Your reason needs to be passionate. It's never your premier book that matters. It's your sophomore book that matters. Your second, third, and fourth books, those will determine whether or not you're an author.

If the reason you're writing the book is because you want to put it in print form to capture what you do, I can get behind that. But you don't need a book necessarily to do that. You can do that through blog posts. You can do that through your newsletter. You can do that through a weekly article in a paper. There's a million other ways you can do that. If you're going to write a book, do it from a place of passion. Write a book because you're an artist. Regardless if it's for fiction or nonfiction. But if you're going to write a book, let's keep the good name of the written word out there. Go be an artist."

That is brilliant advice from Christine on writing from a place of passion and expressing your artistry. Being passionate about what you're writing can make such a difference in your commitment to reaching your goals.

Last but not least, Christine shared a tip for anyone who might feel stuck in their writing.

Commit to writing a sentence. Just one sentence. Give yourself permission for it to be the worst sentence ever written.

Just show up and write a sentence.

Honestly, if a sentence is too hard, then write one word. Then take a breath and write another word – preferably connected to the first word, but it doesn't have to be. Then write another one, and then write another one, until you can write a sentence.

Once you have a sentence, try a paragraph. Once you have a paragraph, try a page. Once you have a page, stop worrying about how much you write. Just show up every day and write. Your muse is always there. Your muse doesn't leave, you leave your muse!

Key Takeaway

- Take inspired action to overcome the "Who am I to write a book?" myth.

- If you're going to write a book, write from a place of passion.

- Take action every day on your writing, even if it means just writing one word for that day.

✳✳✳

To learn more about Christine's books, visit her Amazon Author page

Chapter 15

Kirk Nurmi

Writing Without Expectation

K irk Nurmi, a former lawyer, had practiced law for fifteen years when he decided to leave that profession after he was diagnosed with cancer. He attributes the cancer to the stresses and workload he dealt in the years of being a lawyer. He now has a new purpose in serving other lawyers who may be going through burnout and stress to help prevent them from suffering the same fate he did.

You Are Your Best Audience

I asked Kirk, now the author of several books, with my favorite being *Fighting for Yourself: Self-care for Lawyers*, what his inspiration was for writing that book.

I felt inspired to share my message. I practiced law for fifteen years. The stress of it all is what led to cancer entering my life. It really inspired me to help other lawyers deal with stress, whether it's helping them with addiction or preventing addiction. It had been something that was on my mind. Then a couple of lawyer friends of mine, those that are still practicing law, presented their issues to me and their concerns and some of their stress. It really emphasized to me the need to get this book out and to do what I can to help those lawyers out there. Every profession has their stressors, but I was particularly attuned to those of a lawyer.

Kirk had a powerful message to share on the stresses that come with the job. Having experienced the negative impact stress had on his body, Kirk decided to make a transformation. It's difficult to walk away from a profession to which you've dedicated so many years.

Kirk's former work colleagues approached him for guidance on managing the pressure and challenges of being in a law profession. Who better to help them than one of their own? Kirk can relate and communicate to other lawyers in a way that not everyone would be able to. He understands their fears, dreams, worries, and anxieties better than anyone.

That's definitely true. There are a couple things you said that are important. One is that I think I did it for so long but once I got out of it (practicing law), that changed my perspective. Then I could see the result. A stressed-out person, whether or not they're a lawyer, that stress becomes their comfort zone. That hypervigilance becomes your comfort zone.

When you don't have to look at your phone 150 times a day, when you don't have to worry about it, all the stress comes off. It feels different, right? I started gaining that perspective and realizing how much of a role stress was in my life as a lawyer and how that led to cancer.

I've read so many sad stories about lawyers who have committed suicide based on the stress of the job. There are very high suicide rates for young lawyers. There's a lot of debt involved.

People feel trapped, a servant to that debt. I just wanted to do what I could to just kind of offer them my thoughts (in a book). Like with anything in life, whatever book we write or whatever cause we have, we can't shove it down people's throats. We can only write with sincerity, then offer it to them from our hearts and say, "Here it is if you want it."

I asked Kirk if going back to memory lane made it difficult for him to write the book.

Well, yeah there was certainly some [difficulty] because it did take me back to a place that I didn't want to go. It caused some stress thinking about those times. But that was also my motivation. When I recognize that pain I associated with days gone by, I realized that pain was not in days gone by for others. It was a tense thing that they were waking up with. As much as it was a struggle, it was also the source of inspiration to get that message out to those people, to make it available to them, anyway. Riding with that spirit, the book turned into a number one new release, and that was really exciting. The satisfaction comes from knowing that people are reading it.

Creating an Audiobook

Kirk had released an audiobook version of his other book, *Defend your Greatness*, so I asked him to share what that experience was like.

Well, looking back I feel extremely naive because I thought it would be fairly easy creating an audiobook. I went through Audible, which is obviously the main source of audiobooks. I looked at their requirements, and they're pretty extensive. You have to have music, you have to have room tone, and do all this stuff.

You've got to have a commitment of time and resources. I decided, for this book, I really wanted it to be top-notch. There are some videos up on YouTube on how to do everything. I didn't feel comfortable that sitting in my office was really going to produce a good quality. Now, I'm sure that there are people with more skills who could do it, but I actually went into a studio.

It still took a long time just to produce the right quality. It took two or three days in the studio. You can hire people to do it or you can do different things, but I thought, it's my work, it's my feelings, it's my story. I wanted to do it myself. It's a difficult process to do it, but you're rewarded for it.

What a great insight on creating an audiobook.

Because I don't have experience with audiobooks, I asked Kirk if people care whether the audiobook is read by the author or if it even matters.

Like I said, there are narrators that will do that for you. That might be an avenue some people want to pursue if they don't like their voice or they don't want to take the time. But to me, because it was so personal, I wanted to do it that way. It was my personal journey, and I wanted those feelings to transmit out. But I really see how in another situation it's different. I wrote a weight loss book, so would that matter if it was my voice or not? I don't know. It was very formulaic. But when it's a personal journey, that I felt I needed to relay myself.

That was a great point and clarification. Whether you narrate your book yourself or hire a narrator is up to you. It depends on your goal and the resources you have available.

Personally, I prefer reading a physical book over listening to an audiobook; it's just how I process knowledge. However, not everyone has time to sit and read a book.

Some would rather listen to a book while doing other things like walking, running, or commuting to work. Makes total sense. Each of us processes information differently and having options makes your book more accessible.

Writing Without Expectation

I asked Kirk for one last bit of advice or tip for someone who wants to write a book for the first time.

Write it for yourself. Write it for the cathartic impact. They say dance as if nobody's watching, so write as if nobody's ever going to read it. Then you can decide whether or not you're going to share it. There's stuff that I've written that I haven't published. There's catharsis in that. Don't write with restraints.

I love Kirk's advice to write it for yourself. Whether it will get published or not, it doesn't matter, just do it! There are a lot of psychological benefits in expressing and acknowledging your feelings of the past. You might even begin to heal as a result, similar to writing in a journal. In the end, you have a choice on what you do with your writing. This strategy helps take the pressure of your shoulders.

If you write worried about what somebody is gonna think of this or that, about the wording or how you feel about a certain thing, you're never going to write. You have to write what's in your heart. There are going to be critics, and there are going to be people that love it.

Write without expectation.

I think if you write with the expectation that everybody on the planet is going to want to read your story, you're putting pressure on the writing itself and you're putting pressure on the production because you want to connect with all these people. Then you're obsessed with sales and there's a desperation that comes with that. But that doesn't feel good to you as the author and doesn't feel good to those who you want to purchase your book.

Key Takeaways

- Have an inspirational message to share to the world.

- You can create an audiobook as a complement to your print and/or eBook.

- Write as if no one will read what you've written, and then decide later whether you want to publish it or not.

✱✱✱

To learn more about Kirk's book, visit Amazon

Fighting for Yourself!: Self-Care for Lawyers

Chapter 16

Jas Rawlinson

Sharing a Story from Your Perspective

J as Rawlinson is an Australian memoir writer, a book coach, a resiliency speaker, and a best-selling author of the internationally renowned book series *Reasons to Live One More Day, Every Day*. Despite her success, one thing that people may not know about Jas, is that she herself has gone through much adversity and childhood trauma. That's part of what inspired her to write her first book.

Giving Hope to the Hopeless

What was your inspiration for writing your first book?

It all started back in 2016, when I decided to write a book called Reasons to Live One More Day, Every Day, *– which is a collection of stories from both high profile and everyday Australians who have risen above mental illness, trauma, or adversity. After having experienced childhood trauma myself, as well as many other adversities (including the suicide of my Dad when I was eighteen), I really wanted to use my own story as well* *as those of others, to show people that each of us truly can make it through to the other side of adversity. Each story in* Reasons to Live *is written in first-person, and tells the story of how that person moved through their own darkness — as well as their message to others who are still on their healing journey.*

Since then, I've released a second volume (which includes stories from all around the world), and am now working on the third and final volume of stories, which is really exciting. I love being able to help shine a light on people's lived experiences with mental illness and adversity, because I feel that the more we can reduce stigma around brain pain, the more we can empower people to live their best lives.

What a great reason to write a book and share other people's stories of overcoming adversity.

I followed up with Jas to ask why a book about mental illness and Australians surviving them was important for her.

I have personal experience with mental illness. I grew up in a household with a psychologically abusive father who was also sometimes physically abusive to my mom, and from the age of ten, I was severely anxious and depressed. Of course, at that age I didn't know what it was or what it was called; I just knew that I felt very hopeless and alone. Getting through my teenage years was a very long journey, and I often felt very isolated and hopeless.

It wasn't until 2016, just after I'd co-founded one of Australia's first Domestic Violence Memorials, that I began to think about how I could use my experience around family violence and trauma to help more people. Then, suddenly, I had a revelation: "Why don't I write a book?" I'd been advocating around social issues like domestic violence and child abuse for many years, and I could see that at the heart of every social issue and injustice was another common issue: mental illness and trauma.

Suicide prevention wasn't something I'd really talked about at that stage. Yes, I'd lost my own dad to suicide, but I'd never really talked about it publicly. That's when I realized this is a topic that I understand deeply. This is something I need to open up about. Because if someone like me could make it out the other side of so much trauma and pain, then others need to know that they, too, can overcome the same darkness that I once felt was too overpowering.

I want people to know that there is always hope – even if you can't yet see it. If you haven't yet discovered your life purpose, it doesn't mean that you don't have anything to share with the world. It just means that you're still on your journey to finding it.

Reasons to Live *is all about using the power of storytelling to give very real, unfiltered, and authentic experiences and perceptions of exactly how it feels to go through trauma and adversity, and to let them know that they are not alone.*

Why Creativity Is Not Your Friend Without Organization

Completing a book can be an overwhelming task, so I asked Jas to share some strategies she uses to combat these challenges.

It's easy to feel overwhelmed, but having a deep sense of purpose around my writing has helped a lot. Because if I want to help empower people, how can I quit? I knew that every day my book was not out in the world, another person was fighting to keep their head above water, so I needed to get off my butt and get this book finished.

In terms of strategies, one simple thing I did was to set a goal of doing something small every day. It could be as simple as writing down a list of some people across Australia with really interesting stories that I wanted to interview for my book, and then the next day, looking up emails for their PR agents. Then, my task for the next day might be to draft an email. Small, consistent steps.

I also created a spreadsheet with a list of tasks I needed to achieve each week in order to hit my goal of having the book finished in the time frame that I'd set for myself. Every week, I'd make sure I was on track. If there was something I hadn't done the week before, it would get moved to the current week.

For me, this spreadsheet was one of the biggest things that helped me succeed. I'm very big on organization and structure, and if I don't have everything in one place, then it can be easy to feel overwhelmed and lose track of where I am. With a spreadsheet, I can see exactly where I'm up to each day, and I can easily allocate between five and thirty minutes a day to tick off some more action steps towards those goals.

For some projects, especially those that are large or complex, breaking things down into minor tasks to do each day is key to accomplishing your goal. I took the same approach for the interviews in this book.

If you can break the bigger tasks down to small chunks, then writing a book becomes manageable and easier to attain. It's amazing how much progress you can make within a few weeks.

When I'm working with my own book writing clients, we take a similar approach. We structure their key ideas into a draft chapter list, and then begin to flesh each one out. Just having a bite-sized approach and a rough structure that you can tweak later is incredibly helpful.

There's this common misconception of creatives that we're all really spontaneous and we lack direction — but this isn't true for many of us. Personally, I'm a very creative person, but I also know how to support that creativity through structure and discipline. Organization is so important for me. Otherwise, I won't get anything done.

You Are the Author of Your Story

Jas shared some advice for those who don't feel they are good enough to write.

A lot of my clients have this fear that they will be seen as narcissistic for writing a book or sharing this story. Some of the most common questions they ask are, "Will anyone care or even want to read my story? What if people think I'm really up myself?" ("Full of yourself" for those in the U.S.)

My advice is this: everyone has a unique story to share with the world. While many of us go through very similar things in life, the reality is that NO ONE can tell your story from the same perspective that you can.

Someone else may have a very similar idea for a book, but they can't write it from the same lens you can. When you get to the end of your life, do you think you'll be lying there thinking "Geez, I'm glad I never shared my story. So many people might have said it was really boring." I'm going to go out on a limb and say nope. You're more likely to be thinking, "Wow, I really wish I'd written that book. I really wish I'd shared my story. How many people could I have helped or inspired?" If you don't try, you'll never know.

There was a great visual I saw online one day from an entrepreneur I follow. He said something along the lines of "Imagine that you're lying on your deathbed, surrounded by the ghosts of all of your ideas. And as you look at all those goals and dreams, you realize: 'Wow, I had all these ideas; ideas that only I could have brought it to life. But I didn't, and now those dreams die with me.'"

It's incredibly powerful to visualize. The truth is, we've all been given certain ideas, and we've all been given certain life journeys. If you sit back and constantly live in the "I'm not good enough" mentality, then someone else is going to take that idea, and they're going to share it from a perspective that's different to yours. And you know what? Maybe it was your voice, your story, your perspective that was needed the most. Maybe your perspective was the one that could have changed the most lives.

Something I often share with my clients is this: Your life journey is something that people need to hear. It's powerful. It will help so many people, but if you sit back in this place of fear or thinking you're not good enough to share your story, then you will never know. So many people are going to miss out on the unique benefits that they could have gotten from someone like you sharing your work, sharing your story, and sharing your passion. If you've got an idea, you've got to go for it!

That's a good reminder that we all have unique stories and perspectives to share. There are seven billion people in the world and there will never be another person like you who has the same ideas, experiences, or outlook on life.

If you share your story with ten people, maybe not all ten will connect with you. But there will be two or three that will connect deeply with you. There will be something about your story that resonates with them. That's why your story is so important to share. You never know whose life you might change.

I remember speaking about this during an interview with Kevin Hines — a very well-known international suicide prevention speaker and storyteller, who is also a Golden Gate Bridge Survivor. He shared with me about how many people come up to him at his events and start their conversation the exact same way. "I know, you probably don't want to hear my story, because you probably hear these sorts of stories all the time . . ."

They're nervous to share their stories because they feel like they're not good enough. That no one will want to hear. And what Kevin always says to them, is this: "Please, tell me your stories. I want you to come up and share with me. Everyone has a story and I want nothing more than to hear yours."

Like Kevin, I've also witnessed this a lot in my own work. So often, people will come up to me to share their stories, but they always downplay the power of what they have to share. The truth is, no matter who you are or what you've been through, you have something powerful to share with this world. It's important to quiet those voices that tell you that you're not good enough or that nobody wants to hear your life journey. If you've got a powerful story burning inside of you that could help others, no matter how small you think it is, then you need to work towards it — even if it's just for you.

Key Takeaways

- Setting goals and deadlines for yourself is a key in finishing your book.

- Remember that steady progress wins the race.

- You have a unique perspective that could change someone's life.

To learn more about Jas's book, visit Amazon

Reasons To Live One More Day, Every Day: Stories of Triumph from Australians Who Refused to Give into Darkness

Chapter 17

Melissa Ford

Living in Service

You may have faced a lot of challenges in life, especially in your job or career. Maybe you are unfulfilled in your role or you're not finding any joy in it. Maybe you keep running into the same obstacles and frustrations.

This is where Melissa Ford comes in, helping you approach life in a new and inspired way, whether it be helping you with a career transition or even starting a new business. She has gone through it all and now has a thriving coaching business. But even with her successes, book writing was a new area that she struggled with. Just as she helps clients in creating a business, she needed help in writing her book.

The Service Path

As with our previous authors, I was curious to find out why Melissa wanted to write this particular book.

The book covers the last ten years of my coaching journey when I stepped foot on what I call "the service path," which is to serve someone, to help a prospective client before they pay me and make such a difference in their life that either they want to continue to work with me or things have gotten figured out and they don't want to work with me.

I heard about the service path because I hired a coach. His name is Steve Chandler. I've been working with him over the last ten years. This book follows this ten-year journey from when I stepped foot on the path to who I am today. Those two people are completely different.

The book looks at how I learned to value service and how I learned to love learning, so that I could combine those two things to create a prosperous coaching business.

You asked why I wrote the book — I'm a life and business coach, and I work with lots of people who are transitioning careers. I work with people who get bump ups in whatever business they're in or they get some sort of raise. I also work with coaches.

I help entrepreneurs grow their businesses. I've coached so many different people, and I've watched them on their own journeys. A lot of people struggle like I did, and probably not as much as I did. But they're challenged to understand service, to set a fee, to invite somebody to a conversation, to collect their fee. There are just all these unknowns. I wanted to write this book so that people could have something that they could read where I pull back the curtain and let them see what it takes to grow a coaching business because I would have liked a book like that — a book that would have been honest and simple, shared the ups and downs of a coach's journey, had a little bit of humor in it, and gave me some ideas for where I was at. That's why I wrote it.

I also know the value of coaching because I can see what's changed in my own clients' lives. I've seen what's changed in prospects' lives. I know, being coached for the last decade, what's changed in my life. It's been incredible. I wanted to be able to provide a book that will encourage coaches just to stay with it, stay on their path and what they're doing, ask for help, and do whatever they need to do and not give up. That's why I wrote this book.

I connect with this on so many levels. It's so easy to get discouraged, especially as you start a new business or go through a career transition. Both of which I have gone through in my life.

Coaching has changed so much in my life. I've hired a number of coaches the last few years in different areas including career, writing, life, etc. As a result, my life has completely transformed, and I've had so many breakthroughs.

A writing or life coach will help you see your blind spots that you can't see for yourself. They will be that person who tells you what you *need* to hear — not what you *want* to hear.

A good way to make a transformation is to take a course and/or read books that help solve your problem. But if you really want to make a drastic transformation, hiring a writing coach is the best investment you can make in yourself. A writing coach is your specialized guide to help you focus on the important steps in reaching your goals.

Accountability Is Your Key Ingredient

I asked Melissa what the biggest challenge she faced in writing this book was and how she decided on the messaging for it.

Well, I had to treat the book like I treated my journey with learning how to build a coaching business. I had to be a learner. I had to be honest. I had to be open. I had to be willing. I also hired a book coach as I wanted somebody who could guide me along.

In January 2015, I started writing a book, and about eighteen months into that process, I realized I didn't want to write that book.

I let it percolate for about a year, and then I just felt compelled to write this book, Living Service. *I really felt this message. Everybody goes through these ups and downs. Everybody makes mistakes. Everybody's learning. Everybody gets discouraged. Everybody feels that one minute they're killing it and the next minute they're not. Everybody wonders, should I go back to my job? What should I do?*

I started writing again, and about five months into it, I realized I wanted the help of someone who had a heck of a lot more experience writing a book. I wanted another set of eyes on my work. Because you get immersed in it, you almost have tunnel vision. You get a sense you kind of like what you're writing, but you're not sure.

My book coach helped me with that. I had an outline put together, and then she would ask questions such as, "Could you expand on this? Could you tell a story that would actually take these concepts and give them some meat so that people can understand what you're saying?". I really liked that because I wanted this book to be something that would be useful.

112

My book coach shared with me what a story arc is. This helped me because my book is a narrative-driven nonfiction book. Then I just set a schedule, and I went after it and just kept writing, writing, and rewriting. It was very much a labor of love for me.

That was such a great insight that Melissa shared. She realized that even though she is a business coach herself, writing was a new area for her and she needed help. She sought out guidance and somebody to be by her side who not only made her accountable but also gave her insight into ways of improving her writing. As the famous saying goes, "Feedback is the breakfast of champions."

Writing Is a Messy Process

I wondered if Melissa had any writing beliefs that she felt held her back, maybe not feeling good enough or why would anyone listen to her…

Every single one (of the doubts)! I believed "Somebody could write it better than me," "I don't know what I'm doing," and "I'm not gonna finish this".

One thing that my book coach helped me with was my mistaken idea that writing a book should just come easily. As I was writing, it was so chaotic and such a mess at times because it frankly was messy. She just kept saying, "No, you just keep writing".

I had written a chapter for a previous book, so I had some experience with writing being messy and not clear. But now I was going to write a whole book. I realized I better get comfortable with this messiness. It was easier for me to do it because I knew someone was going to look at the mess and say "expand this" or "take this out." That was super helpful. It got easier as it went along, so that I didn't have a problem with it being messy.

Then it also got easier to be able to cut things from the manuscript. Before, I used to have something I'd spend so much time making it look perfect, and then it would get cut. I'd think to myself, "WHAT? You can't cut that!" But it made sense to take it out. It's been a great learning about how things get created.

I like what Melissa said about having to get comfortable being messy. Writing is a messy process from beginning to end. Rarely can you start writing and all the words are beautiful and flow easily. It doesn't work that way.

You might write ten pages and two might be good. The rest you just have to get rid of. It's kind of like digging through dirt to find the golden nuggets. You have to dig and dig through all the dirt and soil. It's messy work until you find a golden nugget that makes it all worthwhile. Writing is the same way. You hash out all your ideas on paper, and in the mess, you will discover ideas worth refining and going deeper on.

I asked Melissa what advice she had in helping someone who's struggling to move forward with their book.

Go have a conversation with someone and get some clarity about "do you really want to do this?" How can you make it more fun? Talk to people who've written books, get some ideas from them. Just talk to a few people and get some clarity for yourself because if you're on the fence, it's going to be challenging to write a book.

For me, I made the decision, I'm going to write this book. I'm going to start it, and I'm going to finish it, no matter what it takes. I'm going to do whatever I need to do, and I'm going to make it happen. That was the intentionality that I brought to it. But if I had been on the fence, I'm sure it wouldn't have been written. So, if you're on the fence, talk to some people, see what's going on. Why are you holding back? But when you decide to go for it, go for it. If it's something you really feel compelled to write about, it's gonna work its way out.

Key Takeaways

- Do not be afraid to edit or delete sections in your writing that don't add value, despite you spending hours working on it. Better to have a little with a lot of gold than a lot with little meaning.

- Get some accountability and feedback on your writing.

- Learn to be comfortable with a messy writing process.

✹✹✹

To learn more about Melissa's book, visit Amazon
Living Service: The Journey of a Prosperous Coach

Chapter 18

Reverend Jennifer McSween

Why Purpose Is the Biggest Driver for Your Book

"To forgive is the highest, most beautiful form of love. In return, you will receive untold peace and happiness."

—Robert Muller

There is nothing more powerful than the act of forgiveness. Our final author, Rev. Jennifer McSween, wrote an entire book about the topic. She is a Spiritual Psychotherapist turned Transformational Author and Course In Miracles Practice Coach.

Forgiveness is not an easy subject to write about because it requires deep reflection into past pain and hurt. After all, how can you teach something you've never gone through yourself?

Book of Forgiveness

I asked Jennifer why she chose to write about this topic.

116

I shared this in the book; writing was never an end in itself. My intention for writing this book was always to be a platform for what I do, which is helping people heal and transform their lives, based on the teachings of "A Course in Miracles."

It is a form of spiritual psychotherapy.

It uses a lot of religious terminology, but the language is redefined. It's very metaphorical. For example, let's take just something as Christianity, the idea of Jesus for Christians. Jesus is the man who died on the cross to whom you're supposed to turn your life. Jesus in "A Course in Miracles" represents God's perfect love, God's one perfect son, which is really what we all are.

The book is about helping us to recognize what we really are as love. What we are here to do is to learn, recognize, practice, extend, and experience only love in all ways. How we go about doing that is looking at those things that seem to take us away from being whole and that make us feel persecuted and challenged, to realize that this is just coming from a place of fear and a lack of understanding.

We can become open to another way of looking at all of these things and letting go of those fears. That's what "A Course in Miracles" refers to as the process of forgiveness, recognizing your misperceptions, and letting them go.

This is what I have been reading about, studying, learning, teaching, practicing, and trying to live as a way of life for almost twenty years. Writing this book was cathartic for me because I truly lived that experience. I had a lot of pain and unhealed issues in my life. I had a lot of things buried that were not addressed because I really didn't know how to let go of the pain. We don't know how to deal with it.

Just look at the way we are told to handle forgiveness. It's about rationalizing, justifying, trying to say, "Okay, well, look at the good that came out of this. Everything happens for a purpose." All that is true, but you still need to heal what it is that you're feeling. You're still hurting, and you keep stuffing it and stuffing it, but that doesn't make it go away.

"A Course in Miracles" shows us how to address those issues. Those painful areas. How to address the things that seem unforgivable. The most painful hurts. The slights. To look at everything from a new perspective.

What a powerful topic to write about.

Forgiveness is a subject many people know at the surface level but do not fully understand it (I'm one of them). There are people living in pain every day because they haven't learned the correct way to forgive so they can move forward and heal.

What I appreciate most about Jennifer's story is that she wrote a book based on her experience and application of the methods that she now teaches to others. There was no need for her to do more research because she already learned enough through the years to write on the subject from her unique perspective.

Signs of An Author Within You

I wanted to find out from Jennifer when she first got the idea to write a book.

The first inclination I had to write this book was about fifteen years ago. I was coming back from a spiritual counselor training program based on the teachings of "A Course In Miracles."

Part of the program includes a three-week in-person session that we did in Kiel, Wisconsin, where we went as a group for in-depth training. I call it "spiritual surgery" because you truly feel like you have been opened up spiritually.

At the end of the program, we were each ordained as metaphysical ministers. On the day of ordination, we were given gifts, different books by the founders and facilitators. One of the books that we had been given is the little book entitled Inner Healing. *It was based on a process similar to "A Course In Miracles" on ways to heal yourself.*

I'm in the airport with a three-hour layover, and I'm reading this book. It was written in such a simple but profound manner. I felt myself thinking, "You know, I would love to write a book exactly like this one day. That was simple yet profound and practical."

At that point, the seed was planted. I even had a packet of sticky notes. I took a little piece, and I wrote:

"I would really like to write a book, something like this one day."

The seed was planted fifteen years ago for Jennifer to write her book. I can't remember when I got inspired to write a book, but during college is when I started reading lots of books both for school and for my own pleasure.

I remember I was always curious about certain authors, like J.K. Rowling or Stephen King, even though I never read any of their books. I wanted to know about them but not necessarily read their work. It's odd thinking about, but that was my sign of the author in me was to come.

What about you?

Can you remember when you got the first inspiration to write a book?

Was it looking through a bookstore and envisioning having your own book there?

Was it when someone close to you said "you should write a book about that . . ."?

You may have had lots of hints and ideas throughout the years to one day write a book.

Start noticing and being aware whenever you get inspiration to write a book.

Decide to Decide

Why did it take you so long to write a book?

I had made a couple of attempts over the years to write, and I realized two things. First of all, you have to write for the right reason. If you're writing from a place of fear and lack, then you will not be able to follow through because you will have challenges and won't know how to handle it.

The other thing, you have to be ready to write what it is you're going to write about, in terms of having in-depth knowledge and understanding of your subject. Some people go research about something and gather a lot of information and put it out there. That wasn't me.

I had to be coming from a place where I had lived this and not from a place of theory. I could not have written my book in the years before, because I had not lived the process yet. The process of healing brought me to the place where I was able to write. This happened about two years prior to my writing the book. I have lived the process that I was able to put into words, which is why I was able to complete the first draft in a short period of time (like in twenty-eight days).

From the moment I decided to write my book, there wasn't one day where I didn't feel like writing.

I look at that entire period from the first line that I wrote to the final line and think, "Who is that person?" I don't know who that person was because before, I would have to trick myself or bargain on ways to try to keep to my commitment.

When the time is right and when you're ready to commit, there is nothing in the way. You're ready. You're coming from this place of authenticity. You're coming from the space of commitment and certainty and truly this desire to just share. Knowing that there are other people who are probably having some kind of pain around this (forgiveness) or they lack understanding of it.

My whole purpose was sharing my message so that people would be healed and helped by it. This is what the book was all about. The moment I realized that this is what I'm going to be doing, it was like nothing else was in the way.

Jennifer is right. Commitment is key to success in anything, especially book writing. I realized over the years that the hardest part will not be writing your book but rather deciding to do it. By that I mean once you decide to write a book and commit to it, everything will start to fall in place and your focus will be on that goal.

Key Takeaways

- Write a book about a subject on which you have experience and can help someone with.

- Be aware of inspiration that nudges you to write your book and act on it.

- The first step to writing a book is making the decision to do it.

To learn more about Jennifer's book, visit Amazon
True Forgiveness: The Proven Path from Pain to Power in 5 Simple Steps

Conclusion

I f there is anything that you get out of reading this book, I hope it is this, you need to have a purpose for your book. Every author I interviewed had a big "why" to write their book, a "why" that was bigger than themselves.

They wanted to make an impact. To leave a legacy. To contribute to humanity in a positive way.

This is so important because in your writing journey there will be tough days where you struggle to write anything, or you get stuck. It is in those moments where fear and doubt creeps in.

You ask yourself questions like, "Why am I even doing this?"

If you don't have a strong answer for that question, you will quickly get demotivated and lose your focus and discipline with your writing

You will easily quit or find an excuse not to do it.

Once you figure out your "why," write it down and read it every day as a reminder to stay focused and determined on your book.

Remember, writing is a marathon and not a sprint. It doesn't matter how you start — it's how you finish that is the most important. Some authors interviewed took a few months to a few years to write a book. There were a few that took even fifteen years before finally deciding to write.

Each author had their own unique experiences, challenges, and perspectives to writing their first book. Embrace the journey and just start where you are.

Writing a book will be one of the hardest as well as one of the most fulfilling things you do in your life. Know that the world needs to hear your message. It wants to read your story. You can make an impact and inspire others into their greatness.

"The best time to start was yesterday. The next best time is now."

— Unknown

About the Author

PETROS ESHETU is the author of the #1 Amazon best-selling book, *The Introvert Immigrants Journey* and is a Book Writing Coach. He helps transformational leaders get a step by step plan to writing their first book.

He is a graduate of the Cor coaching Academy and has studied writing under Joe Vitale. He also holds an MBA from University of Wisconsin-Eau Claire.

Petros has been featured on *Self Publishing School, Kindlepreneuer, The Helen Show, Minneapolis Life Magazine, Up Journey.com, and Thrive Global*.

www.PetrosEshetu.com
eshetu.petros@gmail.com

Made in the USA
Las Vegas, NV
10 January 2021

15657797R00079